Patricia Tueje is a barrister at One Pump Court. She has practised housing law for over 20 years, and prior to becoming a barrister, worked in the statutory and voluntary housing sectors. She is particularly noted for her expertise in homelessness and landlord and tenant in Chambers & Partners UK. She specialises in all aspects of housing, property and related public law, including homelessness, landlord and tenant and leasehold disputes.

Patricia is co-chair of the Housing Law Practitioners' Association, and a member of the Bar Council's Race Training Delivery Panel.

A Practical Guide to Security of Tenure in the Social Housing Sector in England

A Practical Guide to Security of Tenure in the Social Housing Sector in England

Patricia Tueje

Law Brief Publishing

Published 2023 by Law Brief Publishing, an imprint of Law Brief Publishing Ltd
30 The Parks
Minehead
Somerset
TA24 8BT

www.lawbriefpublishing.com

Paperback: 978-1-914608-70-4

PREFACE

Prior to the Housing Act 1980, there was no statutory provision regulating the types of tenancies or licences social landlords could grant to occupiers. Today, the Housing Acts 1985, 1988 and 1996 govern security of tenure in the social housing sector. Local authority landlords may grant secure periodic, fixed term or flexible tenancies. They may also grant secure licences, introductory tenancies, and apply to the court for a demoted tenancy. Other social landlords may grant assured or assured shorthold tenancies.

This book provides a practical guide to the increasingly complex area of security of tenure in the social housing sector. It explains the requirements for creating the most common types of tenancies granted by social landlords, and the fundamental aspects of the occupiers' security. It focusses on the main grounds and key issues that most frequently arise in possession claims brought by the providers of social housing against their occupiers. It covers all stages of proceedings starting with pre-action conduct, such as compliance with the relevant pre-action protocol, notice requirements and review procedures, through to enforcement, emphasising aspects that are unique to social housing providers.

All reasonable endeavours have been used to ensure the contents of this book accurately reflects the law as it applies to England as at 26th April 2023.

Patricia Tueje
April 2023

CONTENTS

CHAPTER ONE

BACKGROUND

1 – DEFINING SOCIAL HOUSING

Social housing refers to low cost rented accommodation let by local authorities. It also refers to low cost rented accommodation let by Private Registered Providers of Social Housing ("PRPSH"), acting in a public capacity.[1] Accommodation is low cost if it is below market rent.

Social housing law combines elements of public law and private law. On the one hand, social landlords are exercising their public functions to provide accommodation to individuals in housing need. However, it is provided in the context of the traditional private law rights and obligations imposed by landlord and tenant law.

As housing, particularly social housing, has become increasingly scarce, security of tenure in social housing has evolved. It has shifted from rolling lifetime tenancies, that could even sometimes extend beyond a tenant's lifetime to their successor. Instead, social housing tenancies now tend to provide less security, and are increasingly granted as fixed-term tenancies.

The established longer-term tenancies and more recent less secure tenancies co-exist alongside one another. This has increased the range of tenancies in the social housing sector. It has also increased the ways in which social housing tenancies can be brought to an end. Further change may be on the horizon: it's unclear whether or when paragraph 7 of

[1] Some PRPSHs also rent properties at a market rent; the term social housing doesn't apply to those tenancies.

schedule 4 to the Housing and Planning Act 2016 may come into force. If it does, it will phase out lifetime tenancies.

This book deals with the security of tenure of the following tenancies and licences:

- Secure periodic tenancies;
- Flexible secure tenancies;
- Introductory tenancies;
- Non-secure tenancies and non-secure licences;
- Assured periodic and fixed term tenancies; and
- Assured shorthold tenancies.

2 – DEFINING SECURITY OF TENURE

Security of tenure refers to the amount of legal protection an occupier has to remain in their home. It reflects what options, if any, an occupier has to resist a landlord's attempt to recover possession of a property. Most occupiers can resist possession on technical grounds. So a tenant may rely on a technical defence if a landlord makes a procedural error, such as failing to give proper notice. An occupier with greater security of tenure is more likely to have the additional option of raising a substantive defence. So instead of focussing on the procedure, a substantive defence attacks the reasons possession is sought.

The amount of security of tenure an occupier enjoys will depend on a variety of factors, including which, if any, legislation governs their occupation.

A statutory framework providing security of tenure for local authority tenants was first introduced by Chapter II of the Housing Act 1980. It created secure tenancies which at that time were granted to both local authority and PRPSH tenants.

PRPSHs were previously known as Registered Providers of Social Housing, and prior to that known as Housing Associations.

Chapter II of the Housing Act 1980 has been replaced by the Housing Act 1985. This also originally applied to both local authority and PRPSH tenancies. However, the Housing Act 1988 introduced assured tenancies, which have been granted to new PRPSH tenants since then. Local authority tenants remain secure tenants under the Housing Act 1985.

CHAPTER TWO

OCCUPIERS' STATUS

3 – TENANCY OR LICENCE

Another factor affecting security of tenure is whether an occupier has a tenancy or a licence.

Occupiers in the social housing sector generally have more protection than those in the private rented sector. Furthermore, there is no material difference in security of tenure between a secure tenant and a secure licencee. As a result, disputes about whether an occupier is a tenant or licencee arise more often in the private sector.

However, an occupier's status may still be relevant in the social housing sector. Particularly in cases where the local authority wants to evict an occupier without first obtaining a court order. The local authority may not do so with a non-secure tenant, but may sometimes do so with a non-secure licencee. Therefore, the occupier's status could have a significant impact on procedure for evicting them.

Tenancies and licences can be created orally or in writing, but it's unlikely a social housing landlord would grant these orally.

A tenancy agreement gives the tenant a legal interest in the land. This contrasts with a licence, which is a personal right, granting permission to occupy a property.

4 – THE HALLMARKS OF A TENANCY

In most cases, where all the hallmarks of a tenancy are present, it is likely a tenancy has been created. The words used to describe the agreement are not the deciding factor where the description is inconsistent with the facts. Therefore, an agreement described as a licence may nonetheless create a tenancy if all three hallmarks of a tenancy are present.

The hallmarks of a tenancy are firstly, that the occupier has exclusive possession of the property; secondly occupation is granted in return for the payment of rent; and thirdly, occupation is granted for a term.

Exclusive occupation means the occupier has a right to occupy the property, and to exclude all others from the property. This right includes the right to exclude the landlord or the landlord's representative. It means they may only enter the property with the occupier's permission.

The payment of rent reflects it is a formal agreement, by which the landlord allows the tenant to occupy on the payment of, or in consideration of, the rent. This formality is consistent with the tenant having an estate in land. It also distinguishes it from an informal arrangement, for instance where someone stays as a guest.

A tenancy must be granted for a term; the term can either be for a fixed term or periodic. With a fixed-term agreement, the parties expressly agree that the fixed term will last for a specified (i.e. fixed) time. When a fixed-term agreement expires, the tenancy continue as a statutory periodic tenancy if it has not been brought to an end by the parties. In other words, the tenancy rolls over into a statutory periodic tenancy. The statutory aspect relates to the relevant statute which governs the tenancy agreement.

Both the Housing Act 1985 and 1988 make provision for tenancies continuing as statutory periodic tenancies when the initial fixed term expires. The term of a statutory periodic tenancy relates to the period of the rent payments due under the initial fixed-term tenancy. So, where the fixed-term tenancy required rent is paid weekly, on expiry, the tenancy becomes a weekly statutory periodic tenancy, running from week to week.

A tenancy may be granted as a periodic tenancy from the start, so it will simply be a periodic tenancy not a statutory periodic tenancy. The term of a periodic tenancy also relates to the period of the rent payments. Therefore, it would be a weekly periodic tenancy where the rent is payable weekly, and a monthly periodic tenancy if rent's payable monthly.

For example, where the rent is due every Monday in respect of a weekly tenancy, Monday is the first day of the period of the tenancy, and Sunday would be the last day of the period of the tenancy. At common law, where a notice to quit is served, it should expire on the last day of the period of the tenancy.

5 – LICENCES

The most common type of licence is a bare (i.e. non-contractual) licence for resident household members. So where a tenant lives with their family, any family members who are not tenants are licencees. In other words, they live at the property because the tenant has granted them a licence allowing them to live there.

The tenant can revoke that licence by withdrawing their permission for the family member to continue living there. In which case, as the family member has no interest in the property, they must leave. If they refuse to leave, they will be trespassing.

As regards social housing, licencees are likely to be contractual licencees. So they will occupy their property under a licence agreement made with the social landlord.

6 – SOCIAL HOUSING TENANCIES WITH SECURITY OF TENURE

There are a variety of tenures amongst social housing tenants, for instance, secure and assured tenancies affording security of tenure. Through to introductory and starter tenancies which provide no substantive security of tenure.

Security of tenure usually only becomes an issue when one party, normally the landlord, wishes to end the agreement. At that stage, identifying the type of tenancy granted is particularly important to understand each parties' rights. This will also determine which statute applies to the tenancy, and determine the procedure for recovering possession.

Depending on which statute applies, the details of the possession procedure for tenants with security of tenure differs. But there are some common features. Firstly, the landlord must have a reason or ground for seeking possession. The ground for possession must be one specified in the relevant legislation as being an available ground on which possession may be recovered. This is referred to as the statutory ground for possession.

If the ground for possession is or includes rent arrears, the landlord needs to comply with the Pre-Action Protocol for Possession Claims by Social Landlords ("the Protocol"). The landlord needs to comply with the Protocol before serving the notice that initiates the possession process. Serving a document refers to delivering a copy of it to another person.

The Protocol sets out the steps that should be taken before a notice is served. After following the relevant parts of the Protocol, a landlord may initiate possession by serving notice. The notice must state the statutory ground being relied on.

If the ground relied on is not rent arrears, the Protocol does not apply. In such cases, the process is normally initiated by the landlord serving notice on the tenant. The notice warns the tenant of the landlord's intention to recover possession. Again, the notice must state the statutory ground being relied on. This provides the tenant with an opportunity to address the reason, where it's possible to do so. For instance, if the landlord's reason is noise nuisance, it gives the tenant a chance to stop future noise nuisance.

After the notice has expired, the landlord may issue possession proceedings.

Some statutory grounds for possession are discretionary. This means even if the ground is proved, before making a possession order, the court must be satisfied it's reasonable to do so. Other grounds are mandatory, which means the court must make a possession order if the landlord has followed the correct procedure. However, in some case a claim on mandatory grounds can be defended if a public law defence is available.

Where a tenant has security of tenure, a landlord may only end their tenancy by obtaining and enforcing a possession order. Unless or until that happens, the tenancy continues.

7 – SOCIAL HOUSING OCCUPIERS WITHOUT SECURITY OF TENURE

Not all occupiers of social housing are tenants, some are licencees. In the private rented sector whether an occupier is a tenant or licencee can be contentious. Where possible, some private landlords may try arguing an occupier is a licencee because they have less security. Their insecurity makes it easier for the private landlord to evict them. A private sector licencee will not have a substantive defence to possession proceedings.

A social landlord may also grant an occupier a licence instead of a tenancy. Some social housing licencees have no substantive security of tenure. But even social housing licencees without security of tenure may nonetheless have a substantive defence to possession proceedings. For instance, they could rely on a public law defence. Public law defences are discussed in more detail at sectionss 58 to 60 below.

There are a number of situations where a local authority may grant a licence rather than a tenancy. For instance, those occupying supported accommodation usually have a licence rather than a tenancy.

Another situation is where local authorities provide short term accommodation, such as where it provides temporary accommodation to homeless applicants. This can be accommodation from the local authorities own housing stock. In this situation, the local authority must notify the tenant that the accommodation is not provided under a secure tenancy. If the local authority does so, the tenancy will not be a secure tenancy unless it later notifies the occupier otherwise.

There is a similar situation where a local authority may provide accommodation to homeless applicants which is also not occupied under a secure tenancy. This happens where the local authority doesn't own the temporary accommodation provided to the homeless applicant. Instead, the local authority rents it from a third party, and then grants the homeless applicant a licence to occupy it. So although the local authority is the immediate landlord, it does not own the property.

Where the above situations arise, a local authority may grant non-secure tenancies or non-secure licences.

A list of tenancies or licences which are granted by a local authority but excluded from secure tenancy status can be found at Schedule 1 to the Housing Act 1985.

8 – TYPES OF LOCAL AUTHORITY TENANCIES

When the 1985 Act was introduced it allowed local authorities to grant secure periodic or fixed-term tenancies. Most local authorities granted periodic secure tenancies. Subsequent legislation has introduced other different types of tenancies. The Housing Act 1996 ("1996 Act") allowed local authorities to grant introductory tenancies. The 1996 Act also introduced demoted tenancies. Where anti-social behaviour was proved, it allowed the court to downgrade the tenant's security. This meant the court ordered the secure tenancy would be substituted with a demoted tenancy.

Relatively few landlords apply for demoted tenancies. Therefore, they are not dealt with in this book. Readers should refer to section 82A of the Housing Act 1985 for further information about demoted tenancies.

More recently, the Localism Act 2011 allows local authorities in England to grant secure flexible tenancies to new tenants. Flexible tenancies are a type of secure fixed-term tenancy.

Where the term secure tenancy is used in this book, unless otherwise stated, it will include both secure periodic and secure flexible tenancies.

9 – SECURE TENANCIES

Local authority social housing tenancies are secure tenancies, governed by the Housing Act 1985 ("1985 Act"). The 1985 Act applies to local authority tenancies, including those tenancies created before it came into force.

The conditions of a secure tenancy must be satisfied for the 1985 Act to apply. Those conditions are that the landlord is a local authority (see section 80 of the 1985 Act), and the tenant is an individual or individuals (see section 81). The tenant must also occupy the property as their only or principal home. If it's a joint tenancy, the condition is satisfied if at least one of the tenants occupies the property as their only or principal home.

Some tenancies and licences may not be secure even if they satisfy the above conditions. Examples are non-secure tenancies and non-secure licences.

An analysis of the conditions for secure tenancy status are set out in sections 10 to 12 below.

10 – ONLY OR PRINCIPAL HOME

The secure tenancy condition to occupy property as an only or principal home is also relevant in succession and alleged subletting cases. But the term "only or principal home" is not defined in any statute. Another way of describing principal home is main home. Whether the requirement has been met is likely to depend on the circumstances of each individual case.

In reality, most social housing tenants only have one home, making it straightforward to establish whether the requirement is met. However, it can be an issue in some cases. It's unlikely a tenant will be treated as occupying a property as their only or principal home if they have removed all their belongings from a property; live full-time elsewhere; and have no intention of returning to a property. In between this scenario and someone who has one home, others may have more than one home for a variety of reasons. In such cases it's necessary to consider which property is their principal home.

Where an individual stays in more than one place, one way to assess which is their only or principal home may be to look at the purpose of occupying each property. An example is someone who works away from home. If they stay in a guesthouse during the week, but return to live with family at the weekend, their principal home is the family home. They will be regarded as occupying the family home as their only or principal home. That's likely to be the case, even if on average more nights are spent in the guesthouse.

Where an individual keeps all or most of their personal belongings, spends their leisure time and/or they eat their meals, may also be relevant when identifying their principal home.

Where there is a dispute about whether a tenant occupies a property as their only or principal home, tenants may rely on paying the utility bills or receiving official post at a particular property. For instance, if their GP or employer record the property as their home address. They may also rely on relatives, friends and neighbours to confirm they live at the property. A social landlord trying to establish whether a person occupies a property as their only or principal home may look at HMRC's records, the DWP's records, council tax records, the electoral roll and records held by credit reference agencies.

Any combination of these factors may be relevant in a particular situation, which is why this should be considered on a case-by-case basis.

11 – IN AND OUT OF SECURITY

There may be fluidity in whether someone occupies a property as their only or principal home. But the tenant condition is satisfied at any time when one, or at least one joint tenant, occupies the property as their only or principal home. While they are so occupying, the tenancy remains secure. However, it will not be a secure tenancy during any period they cease occupying the property as their only or principal home. During the period they cease occupying, they lose their secure tenancy status. Consequently, they also lose the protection afforded by the 1985 Act. This means they will have no substantive security of tenure, and will be a common law tenant.

For instance, someone may move out of a property, clear their belongings, have no intention of returning, and go to live elsewhere. That person would no longer occupy the departed property as their only or principal home. If their living arrangements at the alternative accommodation breakdown, they may return to live at the original property. And on their return, if they occupy it as their only or principal home, their secure tenancy status is restored.

To recover possession from a common law tenant, a social landlord needs to serve a notice to quit. As previously explained, they will no longer have protection under the 1985 Act. Therefore, if the notice to quit expires while the tenant is not occupying the property as their only or principal home, the notice to quit will end their common law tenancy. In this case, the only protection a tenant has would be section 3 of the Protection From Eviction Act 1977 ("the 1977 Act").

By section 3 of the 1977 Act, a residential occupier may remain in occupation until the landlord obtains a possession order against them.

Because protection under the 1977 Act is only available to a residential occupier, it does not apply to someone who has permanently vacated the property. It would be different if they left the property, resulting in a loss of their secure tenancy status, so becoming a common law tenant. Where a notice to quit is served, and it expires during their absence, the notice to quit would end but their common law tenancy. But if they later returned to live at the property, by resuming occupation, they are a residential occupier under the common law tenancy. Therefore, by section 3 of the 1977 Act, their landlord requires a court order to evict them.

12 – RELATIONSHIP BREAKDOWN

In some circumstances, a tenancy can remain a secure tenancy even if the tenant no longer lives at the property. This may happen where there has been a relationship breakdown. If the tenant leaves the property, but their non-tenant spouse or non-tenant civil partner remains, the tenancy may still be secure.

This is topic is dealt with at section 30 of the Family Law Act 1996.

By section 30, the tenancy remains secure if the non-tenant resident spouse or civil partner occupies the property as their only or principal home. This is because their occupation is treated as it the property is being occupied by the tenant-spouse or tenant-civil partner who has left. Therefore, their continued occupation preserves the security of tenure.

However, their occupation only preserves security so long as they remain spouses or civil partners. Once spouses divorce or a civil partnership is dissolved, security of tenure will be lost if the tenant is not occupying the property as their only or principal home.

13 – SUBLETTING

Subletting involves a series of agreements. Firstly, where a landlord grants a tenancy of a property to person X. In this situation, the landlord may also be referred to as the head landlord. Secondly, if X grants a tenancy of the same property to Y, the tenancy between X and Y is a sub-tenancy. But the sub-tenancy must have all the hallmarks of a tenancy as set out at section 4 above. In which case, X becomes the intermediate tenant (sometimes referred to as the *"mesne"*[2] tenant) and Y would be the sub-tenant.

These arrangements would affect X's security of tenure. For instance, if the head landlord is a local authority which granted X a secure tenancy. If X grants Y a sub-tenancy of the whole property, X will lose their status as a secure tenant. This is because X will no longer occupy the property as their only or principal home. As stated above, a tenant who stops occupying a property as their only or principal home temporarily loses security during the period they are not occupying it. But subletting the whole property is different. If a tenant sublets the whole property, this permanently ends the secure tenancy. Once a secure tenancy ends in this way, it cannot become secure again.

Where a tenant sublets their property and loses security of tenure, they will become a common law tenant. So to recover possession, the landlord only needs to serve a notice to quit. If the landlord needs to issue proceedings to recover possession, there is no need to prove a statutory ground for possession. This is because the statutory protection no longer applies. The tenant's only protection is at common law. Therefore, if the landlord follows the correct procedure the court must make a possession order, unless a public law defence is raised.

The situation would be different if the landlord grants X a secure tenancy, and X takes in Y as a lodger. In that situation, X grants Y a licence rather than a tenancy. X retains their security of tenure because they would continue occupying the property as their only or principal home. But note: some tenancy agreements require the tenant obtains their landlord's permission before taking in a lodger. In such cases, a tenant who takes in

---

2 Mesne is pronounced mean.

a lodger without their landlord's permission would be in breach of their tenancy agreement.

14 – SECURE PERIODIC TENANCIES

Most secure tenancies were granted as periodic tenancies as these are most suited to the objective of providing long-term accommodation. The tenancy will remain secure so long as the conditions of a secure tenancy set out above are met. It will also remain secure unless one party takes positive steps to terminate the tenancy. Such steps would include a landlord serving notice, and obtaining and enforcing a possession order.

The periodic secure tenancy offers the greatest security of tenure of all tenancies granted by local authorities. Some other types of local authority tenancies are dealt with below.

15 – INTRODUCTORY TENANCIES

The 1996 Act created a new type of local authority tenancy called an introductory tenancy. The relevant provisions are contained in Part V of the 1996 Act, sections 124 to 133. The provisions came in to force on 12th February 1997. It gives local authorities the option of formally electing, through the local authority's executive, to operate an introductory tenancy regime. Where a local authority does so, subsequent periodic tenancies granted to its tenants, that would previously have been secure, will be introductory tenancies. And most fixed-term tenancies between two to ten years that would have previously been secure, will also be introductory tenancies.

There is an exception even where the local authority has adopted the introductory tenancy regime. The exception applies where, immediately before a new tenancy is granted, the tenant held a social housing tenancy.

If the social housing tenancy was an assured or secure tenancy, the new tenancy will not be an introductory tenancy.

An introductory tenancy provides a trial period or a probationary period. Introductory tenancies typically last for one year. After the probationary period, the introductory tenancy becomes a secure tenancy.

An introductory tenancy normally continues if the tenant moves to alternative social housing during the probationary period. They will remain an introductory tenant if the new landlord also operates an introductory tenancy regime. Or the probationary period continues if the new landlord is a PRPSH that operates a starter tenancy regime. Providing there is no break between the new and previous tenancies, the trial period continues, it does not start again. So the trial period under the new tenancy will be reduced to reflect the duration of the previous introductory tenancy.

However, the one-year trial period can be extended by six months if two conditions are satisfied. Firstly, if the landlord gives the tenant written notice containing certain required information, including that the introductory tenancy will be extended. The notice must be served at least 8 weeks before the original expiry date of the introductory tenancy. The second condition is the tenant doesn't request a review of the decision to extend the introductory tenancy. Or any review that is requested is dismissed.

A tenant seeking a review of the decision to extend must request it within 14 days of the notice being served. The request doesn't have to be in writing. But it would be advisable for the request to be made in writing. The tenant can therefore confirm the request was made and the date it was made.

The review procedure is set out in the Introductory Tenancies (Review of Decisions to Extend a Trial Period) (England) Regulations 2006.

The regulations state the review will be conducted without an oral hearing unless the tenant requests one. Any request for an oral hearing must also be made within the same 14-day period for requesting a review.

The landlord must give the tenant at least 10 clear days' notice of the review. If there will be an oral review hearing, the landlord must notify the tenant of the time and place of the hearing.

The review must be conducted by someone not involved in making the original decision to extend the introductory tenancy. The person conducting the review must also be senior to the original decision maker.

If there is an oral hearing the tenant may be accompanied or represented. They may be represented by someone who is or is not legally qualified. The tenant or their representative, may call evidence, and question anyone who gives evidence.

The hearing may proceed in the tenant's absence if they have been given notice of the hearing, but they do not attend.

If the applicant requests the review hearing is postponed the landlord may agree or refuse the request. If it's postponed, the tenant must be given reasonable notice of the date, time and place of the postponed hearing.

A tenant may make written representations in support of their review. Any written representations must be received by the landlord at least 2 clear days before the review.

Any written representations made must be considered when reaching the review decision.

Like a secure tenancy, a landlord can only end an introductory tenancy by obtaining a court order which is then executed. But compared to a secure tenant, the process for obtaining a possession order against an introductory tenant is more straightforward. Recovering possession from an introductory tenant is dealt with at sections 26 to 28 below.

16 – FLEXIBLE TENANCIES

Like introductory tenancies, it can be more straightforward to recover possession from a flexible tenant compared to a periodic secure tenancy. Therefore, local authorities are better able to manage housing stock.

Flexible tenancies are dealt with at sections 107A to 107E of the 1985 Act.

To be a flexible tenancy, the tenancy must be granted for a fixed term of two years or more. Also, before granting the tenancy, the local authority must serve a written notice on the person who will be the tenant. The written notice must state the tenancy will be a flexible tenancy. It must also state the other express terms of the tenancy.

If the tenancy being granted is an introductory tenancy, the written notice must also state the following:

- It will become a flexible fixed-term tenancy when the introductory tenancy expires.
- It must state the length of the fixed-term.
- It must state the other express terms of the tenancy.

A landlord's decision to offer a flexible tenancy can be reviewed. A person who is served with a written notice that their tenancy will be a flexible tenancy has the right to request a review. However, any review will only consider the length of the fixed term being offered. Even then, it may only consider whether the length of the fixed term offered is inconsistent with the local authority's policy regarding flexible tenancies. That means there is no right to a review of the decision to offer a flexible tenancy rather than a secure tenancy.

The review must be requested within 21 days of receiving the offer or the written notice. However, the local authority may agree in writing to a longer period. Where a review meeting these requirements is requested, the local authority must provide a written review decision. If the review decision confirms the original decision to offer a flexible tenancy, the local authority must also give reasons for its decision.

There is an exception in the case of those who have experienced domestic abuse. Local authorities are prevented from granting flexible tenancies to those who have experienced domestic abuse in the situations set out below.

The first situation is:

- Where a person has or had a qualifying tenancy, either as a sole or joint tenant.
- The local authority is satisfied the tenant or a member of their household is experiencing or has experienced domestic abuse.
- And a new tenancy for alternative accommodation is granted for reasons connected to the domestic abuse.

The second situation is:

- Where a person has or had a qualifying tenancy, either as a sole or joint tenant.
- The local authority is satisfied the tenant, or a member of their household is experiencing or has experienced domestic abuse.
- And a new tenancy for the same accommodation is granted for reasons connected to the domestic abuse.

A qualifying tenancy is typically a secure tenancy or a PRPSH assured tenancy.

Section 150 of the Localism Act 2011 requires all local housing authorities to prepare and publish a tenancy strategy. Amongst other matters, the tenancy strategy must deal with the following:

- The types of tenancies the authority will grant.
- The circumstances in which it will grant a particular type of tenancy.
- If it will grant fixed-term tenancies, the length of the terms that will be granted.
- The circumstances in which a further tenancy will be granted when the fixed-term tenancy expire.

The tenancy strategy must be kept under review, and it may be amended from time to time or replaced as appropriate.

Early indications were that flexible tenancies were not particularly popular in the years following the introduction of the Localism Act. For instance, as at September 2018, 29 of 50 English local authorities did not support using flexible tenancies[3]. However, it's anticipated in time the number of local authorities using flexible tenancies is likely to increase.

Furthermore, legislation has been passed, but is not yet in force, which phases out secure periodic tenancies (see paragraph 7 of schedule 4 to the Housing and Planning Act 2016). If that legislation comes into force, new local authority tenancies will be flexible tenancies.

3 Social housing: flexible and fixed-term tenancies (England) (parliament.uk) – https://researchbriefings.files.parliament.uk/documents/CBP-7173/CBP-7173.pdf

17 – NON-SECURE TENANCIES AND LICENCES

There is no statutory definition of a non-secure tenancy or non-secure licence.

A non-secure tenancy arises where the landlord and tenant conditions required for a secure tenancy are met (see sections 80 and 81 of the 1985 Act). The hallmarks of a tenancy are present, but for some reason, the tenancy created is not a secure tenancy. For instance, the tenancy may be excluded from secure tenancy status under Schedule 1 to the 1985 Act. One situation where a non-secure tenancy arises is where a local authority temporarily rehouses a secure tenant while repairs are carried out at the tenant's home.

A non-secure licence arises where the landlord and tenant conditions required for a secure tenancy are satisfied. If the agreement creates a licence, it will be a non-secure licence if it is excluded by law from protection under the 1985 Act. This may happen where a local authority provides interim accommodation to a homeless applicant.

18 – TENANCIES GRANTED BY PRIVATE REGISTERED PROVIDERS OF SOCIAL HOUSING

Like local authorities, historically PRPSHs granted tenancies that were intended to be lifetime tenancies. In fact, prior to 15th January 1989 PRPSHs granted secure tenancies.

However, due to the scarcity of social housing, tenancies granted by PRPSHs now tend to provide less security. As a result, the use of fixed-term tenancies by PRPSHs has increased in recent years. This coincided with, and was undoubtedly influenced by, the regulatory framework for social landlords published when the Localism Act 2011 was introduced. At that time, it was published by the Homes and Communities Agency

("HCA"). The HCA has since been replaced by the Regulator of Social Housing ("RSH").

The regulatory framework requires general needs [4] secure or assured tenants are granted periodic tenancies, or tenancies for a minimum fixed term of five years. Or exceptionally, a fixed term tenancy for a minimum of two years, in addition to any probationary period.

The regulatory framework also sets out the Tenancy Standard PRPSHs are required to meet. The regulatory framework is periodically updated. It's guidance on tenure is similar to the provisions at section 150 of Localism Act 2011 regarding local authority tenancy strategies (see section 16 above). It means that where PRPSHs grant fixed-term tenancies, this should be dealt with in their tenancy strategies.

In relation to security of tenure, the Tenancy Standard states a PRPSH's tenancy strategy needs to deal with the following:

- The types of tenancies the PRPSH will grant.
- The circumstances in which it will grant a particular type of tenancy.
- If it will grant fixed-term tenancies, the length of the terms that will be granted.
- The circumstances in which a further tenancy will be granted when the fixed-term tenancy expire.
- The mechanism for an individual to appeal against or complain about a fixed-term tenancy. The mechanism should allow an appeal or complaint to be made on the following grounds:

---

[4] General needs tenants are those who are not in supported housing

- The fact that a fixed-term tenancy is being offered.
- The length of the fixed-term.
- The decision not to grant a further tenancy when the fixed-term expires.

Section 19 considers assured tenancies granted by PRPSHs, and section 20 considers assured shorthold tenancies.

19 – ASSURED TENANCIES GRANTED BY PRIVATE REGISTERED PROVIDERS OF SOCIAL HOUSING

PRPSH tenancies created before 15th January 1989 are governed by the Housing Act 1985. Therefore, sections 9 to 13 above apply to these tenancies.

Most PRPSH tenancies created after 15th January 1989 are governed by the Housing Act 1988.

The 1988 Act created assured tenancies (see section 1). There are two types of assured tenancies: (fully) assured tenancies providing security of tenure; and assured shorthold tenancies which provide no substantive security of tenure.

When a tenancy is created under the 1988 Act, the default position is that it will be an assured shorthold tenancy. For this reason a PRPSH that wants to grant an assured tenancy must serve a notice under section 19A of the 1988 Act before the tenancy begins, stating it will be an assured tenancy.

This book only deals with assured and assured shorthold tenancies granted by social landlords. But because the 1988 Act also governs most private sector tenancies some of its provisions tend to suit that sector. For instance, from the outset the 1988 Act also included mandatory grounds for possession in relation to assured tenancies. These are grounds 1 to 8 of schedule 2 to the Housing Act 1988. It means PRPSHs are providing social housing within a legislative framework that also applies in the private rented sector.

Over the years, the number of mandatory grounds available to social landlords have increased. This is because the ASBCP Act 2014 introduced into the 1988 Act a new mandatory ground for possession. The new ground was inserted at paragraph 7A of Schedule 2 to the 1988 Act. It is based on criminal convictions or proven anti-social behaviour.

The main difference between the requirements necessary to create an assured tenancy and a secure tenancy are the identity of the landlord. With a secure tenancy, the landlord condition must be fulfilled. There is no corresponding landlord condition with assured tenancies, although some bodies, such as the Crown, cannot create an assured tenancy.

A list of situations in which an assured tenancy cannot be created can be found at Schedule 1 to the 1988 Act.

Apart from the identity of the landlord, the requirements to create an assured tenancy are broadly similar to a secure tenancy.

The requirements can be summarised as follows:

- The tenant or tenants must be individuals.

- The tenant must occupy the property as their only or principal home. Or, if it's a joint tenancy, at least one must occupy the property as their only or principal home (see section 10 above).

- All three hallmarks of a tenancy must be present (see section 4 above).

- An assured tenancy may come in and out of security (see section 11 above).

- Subletting the whole of the property will permanently end the assured tenancy (see section 13 above).

20 – ASSURED SHORTHOLD TENANCIES GRANTED BY PRIVATE REGISTERED PROVIDERS OF SOCIAL HOUSING

A number of PRPSHs have implemented the guidance in the RSH's Tenancy Standards (see section 18 above) by using fixed-term assured shorthold tenancies.

This represents a departure from the previous widespread use of assured tenancies. These assured shorthold tenancies are typically granted for 5 years, and therefore are in accordance with the RSH's Tenancy Standards. This is because the RSH recommends that where fixed term tenancies are granted, they are for a minimum 5-year term. These provide less security of tenure than traditional assured periodic tenancies. It means these PRPSH tenancies more closely resemble private sector tenancies. For instance a landlord can evict an assured shorthold tenant without proving a statutory ground. Obtaining possession is largely procedural: ensuring the correct notice is properly served in accordance with section 21 of the 1988 Act.

However, some PRPSHs still rely on section 8 and schedule 2 of the 1988 Act to recover possession from assured shorthold tenants on discretionary grounds. And some PRPSHs that bring mandatory possession claims (i.e. under section 21, or grounds 1 to 8) operate a review procedure. These tend to be similar to the review procedure local authorities adopt when they intend to recover possession from introductory tenants. Where available, reviews give assured shorthold tenants the opportunity to challenge the decision to seek possession on mandatory grounds. It also means when properly conducted, carrying out a review, may insulate PRPSHs against public law challenges.

Except that a section 19A notice isn't needed, all other requirements to create an assured shorthold tenancy are the same as to create an assured tenancy. The requirements are set out at section 19 above.

The main difference between an assured and an assured shorthold tenancy is the security of tenure. This means, while creating each type of tenancy is broadly similar, recovering possession from an assured shorthold tenant is more straightforward if the correct procedure is followed.

The Renters' Reform Bill is expected to be published shortly. An important feature of the proposed legislative reform is the repeal of section 21. If this becomes law, it's anticipated a new tenancy regime will replace assured and assured shorthold tenancies in their current form.

CHAPTER THREE

INITIATING POSSESSION

21 – PRE-ACTION PROTOCOL (DISCRETIONARY GROUNDS)

The Ministry of Justice has published a Pre-Action Protocol for Possession Claims by Social Landlords ("the Protocol"). The Protocol applies in rent arrears claims. It aims to encourage meaningful exchange between social landlords and their tenants. Where possible, these exchanges are intended to resolve matters without the need for court action.

The Protocol deals with conduct before notice seeking possession is served. It also deals with the period after service of the notice but before proceedings are issued. The Protocol is not mandatory. But the court can take a landlord's non-compliance in to account when deciding what order, if any, to make.

Part 2 of the Protocol deals with discretionary rent arrears claims. It sets out the various steps a landlord should take.

Those steps include:

- Making timely contact with the tenant to discuss the cause of the arrears, their finances, and potential welfare benefit entitlement.

- Offering to assist the tenant with benefit claims, including by contacting the relevant department or agency on the tenant's behalf.

- Trying to agree repayment of the arrears by affordable instalments.

- Where the relevant criteria is met, those instalments should be paid by direct deductions from the tenant's benefits. If so, the landlord should apply to the Department of Work and Pensions to facilitate this.

The Protocol recommends proceedings should not be started where the following apply:

- The tenant can show a reasonable prospect of welfare benefit assistance with their housing costs.

- The welfare benefit claim and the necessary information to support the claim has been submitted.

- The tenant has paid sums not covered by benefits.

After notice has been served the landlord should contact the tenant and provide them with a copy of the Protocol. If the tenant agrees to repay the arrears by reasonable instalments, proceedings should not be issued so long as the tenant complies with that agreement. If the tenant stops complying, the landlord should warn them of the timescale within which proceedings will be issued.

22 – SECURE TENANCY GROUNDS FOR POSSESSION

Where a local authority landlord wishes to evict a secure periodic tenant, it may only do so by relying on one or more specific grounds or reasons. The specified grounds are set out at schedule 2 to the 1985 Act. There are currently 20 statutory grounds for possession available under the 1985 Act. By far the grounds most frequently relied on are rent arrears (ground 1), which also deals with other tenancy breaches, and anti-social behaviour (ground 2).

Until October 2014 only discretionary possession grounds were available to a local authority landlord. To rely on a discretionary ground the landlord must first prove the ground is made out. Additionally, the landlord must satisfy the court that it is reasonable to make a possession order.

This changed on 20th October 2014 when the Anti-Social Behaviour, Crime and Policing Act 2014 ("ASBCP Act 2014") came into force. The ASBCP Act 2014 introduced into the 1985 Act a new ground for possession. The new ground was inserted at section 84A of the 1985 Act. It is based on proven criminal or anti-social behaviour. The new ground is not discretionary, it's a mandatory ground, which is sometimes referred to as an absolute ground. So far it is the only absolute/mandatory ground for possession available against a secure tenant.

23 – NOTICE RELYING ON DISCRETIONARY GROUNDS

In almost all cases where a landlord wishes to recover possession it must serve on the tenant a notice seeking possession under section 83 of the 1985 Act. Although the court may dispense with the requirement to serve a notice in relation to any discretionary ground. But the court will only dispense with the requirement if it is just and equitable to do so.

The notice served must state the landlord's ground (or reason) for seeking possession.

In some cases a landlord may be required to serve notice seeking possession on a non-tenant. This is where the ground or one of the grounds relied on is ground 2A.

Ground 2A applies where:

- The property was occupied by a couple.
- The couple are spouses, civil partners, or were living together as if they were spouses or civil partners.
- Either or both were tenants.
- One of them has left the property.
- They left because of violence or threats of violence from the other spouse, civil partner or equivalent partner.
- The violence or threats of violence were towards the partner who has left or a member of that partner's family who lived with them.
- And the court is satisfied that the partner who has left is unlikely to return.

In such a case, a local authority may rely on ground 2A to try to evict the partner still living at the property. If it does so, the landlord should also serve notice on the partner who left, even if they are a non-tenant. If the landlord cannot serve notice on the partner who left, it must at least have taken all reasonable steps to try to serve them.

Only the statutory grounds for possession due to rent arrears and anti-social behaviour are discussed in this book. As stated, these are the most common grounds.

The rent arrears ground is ground 1 at schedule 2 to the 1985 Act, which reads:

> *Rent lawfully due from the tenant has not been paid or an obligation of the tenancy has been broken or has not been performed.*

The discretionary anti-social behaviour ground is ground 2 at schedule 2 to the 1985 Act, which states:

The tenant or a person residing in or visiting the dwelling house-

(a) *has been guilty of conduct causing or likely to cause a nuisance or annoyance to a person residing, visiting or otherwise engaging in lawful activity in the locality,*

(aa) *has been guilty of conduct causing or likely to cause a nuisance or annoyance to the landlord of the dwelling house, or a person employed (whether or not by the landlord) in connection with the exercise of the landlord's housing management functions, and that is directly or indirectly related to or affects those functions, or*

(b) *has been convicted of-*

(i) *using the dwelling-house or allowing it to be used for immoral or illegal purposes, or*

(ii) *an indictable offence committed in, or in the locality of the dwelling house.*

Where notice is served, it must be in the prescribed form. The form can be found at Part I of the Schedule to the Secure Tenancies (Notices) Regulations 1987. The notice must specify the ground or grounds relied on, and give the particulars of each ground relied on. If the tenancy agreement imposes additional requirements on the landlord relating to serving notices, these must also be complied with. For instance, a tenancy agreement may restrict the landlord to seeking possession only on certain statutory grounds. Or it may require the notice given is longer than the statutorily required notice period. But any terms which try to restrict a tenants statutory rights relating to possession will be ineffective.

The court will also require evidence that the notice has been served. This is usually provided by a witness statement containing all relevant information regarding service. Or evidence can be provided by completing the N215 court form called a Certificate of Service.

Many written tenancy agreements deal with any notice relating to the tenancy that are served by the landlord. The agreements may state notices will be treated as properly served if certain requirements are fulfilled. For instance, the tenancy may state notices sent by special delivery or first-class post will be treated as properly served. Where a tenancy agreement contains such a clause, the landlord only needs to prove that it has complied with that clause. Meaning there will be proper service if the landlord complies with the requirements in the tenancy agreement, even if the tenant does not receive the notice.

Different notice periods apply depending on which ground is relied on. Where the ground or one of the grounds relied on is ground 2, the notice must state proceedings may be brought immediately. It must also specify the date by which the tenant should vacate the property.

Where ground 2 is not relied on, a longer notice period applies. Such notices must specify the date after which possession proceedings will be brought. That date must not be earlier than the date on which a notice to quit would expire (see section 32 below).

In either case, the notice is valid for 12 months from the date specified in the notice as the date after which possession proceedings will be brought.

24 – NOTICE RELYING ON THE ABSOLUTE GROUND

Where possession is sought on the absolute ground, sections 83ZA and 84A of the 1985 Act apply.

Section 83ZA deals with the notice requirements where the absolute ground is relied on.

The requirements are that the notice must state:

- The court will be asked to make an order for possession under section 84A.
- The landlord's reasons for seeking possession.
- Which of the condition or conditions in section 84A apply.
- Inform the tenant that under section 85ZA they have the right to request a review, and the timescale for requesting a review, of the landlord's decision to seek possession on this ground.
- The date after which proceedings may be brought, which must not be earlier than the date a notice to quit would expire.
- That the notice is valid for 12 months from the date specified as the date after which possession proceedings will be brought.
- And that the tenant should take the notice to a Citizens' Advice Bureau, housing aid centre, law centre or solicitor immediately, if they need advice.

The above requirements apply whether the absolute ground is relied on alone, or with other grounds for possession. Therefore, if other grounds are also relied on the landlord should comply with the requirements under section 83ZA rather than section 83 of the 1985 Act.

Notice under this ground cannot be dispensed with. The court will also require evidence that the notice has been served. And because the notice cannot be dispensed with, evidence of service is particularly important.

Section 84A sets out the conditions which must be satisfied where the absolute ground is relied on. The absolute ground may only be relied on where at least one of the five conditions is met.

In summary, the conditions are as follows:

- Condition 1 – A conviction of a serious offence.
- Condition 2 – A court finding that an injunction granted under ASBCP Act 2014 has been breached.
- Condition 3 – A conviction under section 30 of ASBCP Act 2014 or under section 339 of the Sentencing Code.
- Condition 4 – A closure order has been made in respect of the property.
- Condition 5 – A conviction under section 80(4) or 82(8) of the Environmental Protection Act 1990.

There are additional notice requirements depending on which of the five conditions under section 84A is being relied on.

Where the landlord relies on conditions 1, 3 or 5, the notice must state the conviction being relied on. The notice must also be served within 12 months of that conviction.

Where the landlord relies on condition 2, the notice must state the court finding being relied on. Again, the notice must be served within 12 months of that finding.

Where the landlord relies on condition 4 the notice must state the closure order concerned. The notice must be served within 3 months of the closure order being made.

The period within which notice must be served is subject to whether the tenant appeals the conviction, finding or closure order. If the tenant appeals, the relevant period for serving the notice begins on the day the appeal is determined, abandoned or withdrawn.

Where the section 83ZA notice specifies any other ground for possession, the notice must give particulars of those ground.

25 – REVIEW OF A LANDLORD'S DECISION TO RELY ON THE ABSOLUTE GROUND

A tenant has the right to request a review of a landlord's decision to recover possession on the absolute ground. A tenant who wishes to do so, must request the review in writing within 7 days of the notice being served. The landlord must give the tenant its review decision before the notice expires. The review decision must be in writing. If it confirms the original decision, the landlord must provide reasons for its decision.

The review procedure is set out in the Absolute Ground for Possession for Anti-social Behaviour (Review Procedure) (England) Regulations 2014 ("the 2014 Regulations"). It sets out the timescale for each stage of the review process, and how it should be conducted. It also states the review must be conducted by someone not involved in making the original decision, and they must be senior to the decision maker.

In summary, the 2014 Regulations state, when requesting a review, the applicant must provide certain specified information including:

- The applicant's name and address;
- The date and a description of the decision being reviewed;
- The reasons or grounds for seeking a review;
- Confirmation as to whether the review should or should not be conducted by an oral hearing;
- Whether the applicant agrees to receiving communications by e-mail, and if so the applicant's e-mail address.

If the applicant opts for an oral review hearing, the landlord must provide information about that hearing. The landlord must notify the applicant of the date, time and place of the hearing. The applicant must be given at least 5 days' notice of the review hearing. The landlord may postpone the hearing if the applicant requests this before the hearing. The original decision maker may also attend the hearing. At the oral hearing the applicant and the decision maker may be accompanied or represented. The applicant, decision maker or any representative, may make oral or written submissions, call evidence, and question anyone who gives evidence. The person conducting the review must be the person who reaches the review decision.

The hearing may proceed in the applicant's absence if they do not attend. Of if they don't attend, the hearing may also be adjourned if considered appropriate.

Where the review is conducted without an oral hearing the tenant must be notified they are entitled to make written representations. They must be notified of the date by which any written representations must be received. The date for submitting written representations must be at least 5 days after the applicant receives information regarding the review procedure. Any written representations made must be considered when reaching the review decision.

26 – RECOVERING POSSESSION FROM AN INTRODUCTORY TENANT (THE PRE-ACTION PROTOCOL)

An introductory tenant has no substantive security of tenure. Therefore, if a local authority follows the correct procedure before issuing proceedings, the court will normally make a possession order. It means the local authority's reason for claiming possession does not need to be one of the statutory grounds. But where the reason the landlord issues possession proceedings is rent arrears, Part 3 of the Protocol applies.

The Protocol requires the landlord to take certain steps before issuing proceedings.

The first step is the landlord should write to the occupants explaining the reason it intends to issue proceedings. This can be done either before or at the same time the landlord serves a notice seeking possession. Secondly, the landlord should request information from the occupier. The landlord should request the occupier sets out in writing their personal circumstances, and anything the landlord should consider. The landlord should also provide a deadline for the occupier to provide the requested information.

The landlord should consider any information the occupier provides. It should then decide whether to proceed with a possession claim. If it does so, the landlord should give the tenant brief written reasons.

The landlord should provide the court with the information obtained as a result of complying with the Protocol. The information can be provided with the claim form or with the landlord's evidence submitted before the first court hearing.

The information the landlord provides to the court should include the following:

- Whether it gave the defendant an opportunity to make representations about their personal circumstances, or representations about other relevant matters before proceedings were issued.

- If so, how this was done. For instance, by a statutory review or some other procedure.

- How any representations it received were dealt with, and the outcome.

- The landlord's brief reasons for bringing the possession claim.

- Any other documents the landlord considers is relevant to the proportionality of its decision to issue proceedings.

27 – NOTICE OF PROCEEDINGS FOR POSSESSION OF AN INTRODUCTORY TENANCY

Before bringing a claim, the landlord must serve on the tenant a notice of proceedings (see section 128 of the Housing Act 1996). The notice must satisfy the following requirements:

- It must state the court will be asked to make a possession order in respect of the property.

- The notice must set out the landlord's reasons for bringing the possession claim.

- The notice must state the date after which the possession claim may be brought. That date must not be earlier than the date on which a notice to quit would expire.

- It must explain a possession claim cannot be brought until after the date specified in the notice.

- It must inform the tenant of their right to request a review of the landlord's decision to bring a possession claim. It must also explain the time limit for requesting the review.

- It must advise the tenant to take the notice to a Citizens' Advice Bureau, housing aid centre, law centre or solicitor, if they require help regarding the notice.

The court does not have the power to dispense with service of the notice of proceedings. Nor does the court have the power to excuse or waive any defects in the notice of proceedings. Therefore, if a landlord wishes to recover possession from an introductory tenant, it must comply strictly with the notice requirements. If the landlord fails to comply with the requirements, this will provide the tenant with defence to a possession claim.

The procedure that applies if an introductory tenant exercises their right to request a review is set out in section 28 below.

28 – REVIEW OF THE DECISION TO RECOVER POSSESSION FROM AN INTRODUCTORY TENANT

Where an introductory tenant wishes to review the local authority's decision to recover possession, it must be requested within 14 days of receiving the notice of proceedings.

If the tenant requests a review within this timescale, the landlord must review its decision. The review must be conducted by someone not involved in making the original decision to bring a possession claim. They should also be more senior to the original decision maker.

The landlord must notify the tenant of its review decision.

The landlord must give the tenant its review decision before the notice expires. If the review decision upholds the original decision to seek possession, the landlord must provide its reasons.

The review procedure is set out in the Introductory Tenants (Review) Regulations 1997. It sets out the timescale for each stage of the review process, how it should be conducted, and by whom.

In summary, it states:

- The review will be conducted without an oral hearing unless the tenant requests one.

- Any request for an oral hearing must also be made within the same 14-day period for requesting a review.

- Where the review is conducted without an oral hearing the tenant must be notified they are entitled to make written representations.

- They must be notified of the date by which any written representations must be received.

- The date for submitting written representations must be at least 5 days after the applicant receives information regarding the review procedure.

- Any written representations made must be considered when reaching the review decision.

If the tenant opts for an oral review hearing, the landlord must provide information about that hearing. The landlord must notify the applicant of the date, time and place of the hearing. The date of the hearing must be at least 5 days after the applicant receives the notice regarding the review hearing. The landlord may postpone the hearing if the applicant requests this before the hearing.

The oral review hearing must be conducted with minimal formality.

The original decision maker may also attend the hearing.

At the oral hearing the applicant and the decision maker may be accompanied or represented. The representative may or may not be legally qualified.

The applicant, decision maker or any representative, may make oral or written submissions, call evidence, and question anyone who gives evidence. The person conducting the review must be the person who reaches the decision.

The hearing may proceed in the applicant's absence if they do not attend. Or, if they don't attend, the hearing may also be adjourned if considered appropriate.

The person conducting the review must be the person who reaches the decision.

Where the review is conducted without an oral hearing the tenant must be notified they are entitled to make written representations. They must be notified of the date by which any written representations must be received. The date for submitting written representations must be at least 5 days after the applicant receives the notice.

Any written representations made must be considered when reaching the review decision.

29 – RECOVERING POSSESSION WHEN THE FLEXIBLE TENANCY EXPIRES

This section deals with the conditions required to obtain possession when the fixed term of a flexible tenancy has ended. The statutory provisions can be found at sections 107C to 107E of the 1985 Act.

The court must make a possession order if a claim is brought at the end of a flexible tenancy, and the conditions set out below are met.

The first condition is that the fixed term of the flexible tenancy must have ended, and no further tenancy has been granted. So the landlord must not have granted either a secure periodic or a further flexible tenancy. If the tenant continues occupying the property, this will be as a statutory periodic tenant (see section 4 above), and not the grant of a further tenancy.

The second condition is that the landlord has given the tenant at least six months written notice stating:

- The landlord does not propose to grant another tenancy.

- The landlord's reasons for proposing to not grant another tenancy.

- The tenant's right to request a review of the landlord's decision and the timescale for requesting the review.

The third condition is that the landlord must give the tenant at least two months written notice that it requires possession of the property. The two months written notice may either be given before or on the day the fixed term ends.

There is no prescribed form for either of the above notices.

As stated, the above conditions must be met before a landlord can recover possession. If a possession order is made, that order will terminate any statutory periodic tenancy (i.e. any rolling tenancy) that has arisen.

The three conditions do not include a requirement that the landlord carries out any review the tenant may have requested. So the court could still make a possession order if the landlord fails to carry out a review requested by a tenant. The court could also make a possession order if a review is carried out that does not comply with section 107E of the 1985 Act, or is wrong in law in another way. Alternatively, the court could refuse to make an order if a review is requested but there is no review or no lawful review. If the court refuses to make an order it may give directions for the landlord to carry out the review.

30 – REVIEW OF THE LANDLORD'S DECISION PROPOSING TO RECOVER POSSESSION WHEN A FLEXIBLE TENANCY ENDS

As stated, a tenant has a right to a review of the landlord's decision to recover possession when the fixed term of a flexible tenancy ends. The tenant must request the review within 21 days of receiving the landlord's six month notice of its decision to recover possession. There is no requirement that the tenant's request is made in writing. Nevertheless, it's advisable that any such request is made in writing. That way the tenant can confirm the request was made and the date it was made. If a review is requested in time, the landlord must carry out the review. When doing so, the landlord must consider whether the decision to end the tenancy is in accordance with its tenancy strategy.

When the review is completed, the landlord must notify the tenant in writing of its decision. Any adverse written decision must contain reasons. The landlord must also notify the tenant of its decision before the two-month notice requiring possession expires.

31 – RECOVERING POSSESSION DURING THE FIXED TERM OF THE FLEXIBLE TENANCY

Possession can only be recovered during the fixed term of a flexible tenancy where the wording of the tenancy agreement expressly allows this. The wording can be in the form of a contractual break clause or a forfeiture clause.

If the tenancy contains a break clause, the landlord can terminate the fixed term in accordance with the requirements of the break clause. The tenancy will then continue as a periodic tenancy. So the landlord will need to recover possession in the same way as it would against any secure periodic tenant.

Alternatively, the landlord may exercise a forfeiture clause if the tenancy contains such a clause. Forfeiture allows a landlord to re-enter the property where a tenant has breached the tenancy. Re-entry is ordinarily effected by obtaining a forfeiture order from the court allowing re-entry. But that doesn't happen where a flexible tenancy is forfeited. Instead, when an order for forfeiture is made against a flexible tenant, a secure periodic tenancy arises under section 86 of the 1985 Act. To terminate the periodic tenancy that has arisen, the landlord must claim for possession as it would against a periodic tenant.

32 – RECOVERING POSSESSION FROM A NON-SECURE TENANT

A non-secure tenancy is not covered by the Housing Act 1985. Therefore, a non-secure tenancy can be brought to an end by the landlord serving a notice to quit on the tenant.

If the reason for serving notice to quit is rent arrears, the landlord must comply with Part 3 of the Protocol.

The notice to quit must comply with the requirements contained in section 5 of the Protection From Eviction Act 1977.

Section 5 requires a notice to quit complies with the following:

- It must be in writing.
- It must contain prescribed information.
- The prescribed information is set out in the schedule to the Notices to Quit etc. (Prescribed Information) Regulations 1988.
- It must provide the occupier with at least 4 weeks' notice.

In addition to the requirements under section 5, by common law a notice to quit served on a non-secure tenant must also end on the last day of a period of the tenancy (see section 4 above).

Where reference is made elsewhere in this book to the requirements of a notice to quit, it relates to all requirements in the two preceding paragraphs.

A non-secure tenant also enjoys the protection afforded by section 3 of the Protection From Eviction Act 1977. This means where a non-secure tenant remains in occupation after the notice to quit has expired, the social landlord must obtain a court order to recover possession.

As stated, a non-secure tenant cannot rely on the Housing Act 1985 to defend the possession claim. But depending on the circumstances of their case, it may be possible to rely on a public law defence. These are dealt with at sections 58 to 60 below.

33 – RECOVERING POSSESSION FROM A NON-SECURE LICENCEE

Most non-secure licencees do not benefit from section 3 of the Protection from Eviction Act 1977. For instance, where a local authority grants a non-secure licence of hostel accommodation, it is an excluded licence. This means the licence is excluded from the protection afforded by sections 3 and 5 of the 1977 Act. Other non-secure licences are also excluded from the protection of the 1977 Act. For instance, where a local authority grants a non-secure licence to a homeless person to whom the local authority owes an interim duty to accommodate[5]. In such cases, the

[5] This is a duty under section 188(1) of the Housing Act 1996 owed to individuals who have made a homeless application, and the local authority has housed them on an interim basis while it makes enquiries to decide

licence is excluded, irrespective of whether the interim accommodation is in a hostel or self-contained.

Instead of serving a 28-day notice to quit, a non-secure licence can be brought to an end by the landlord giving the tenant reasonable notice. What amounts to reasonable notice will depend on the facts of each case. Where the licence agreement specifies a period of notice, notice shorter than the period specified is unlikely to be reasonable.

In other situations where a non-secure licence is granted, section 3 of the Protection From Eviction Act 1977 will apply. Therefore, the local authority will need to follow the same possession procedure as for non-secure tenants.

34 – NOTICE REQUIRING POSSESSION SERVED BY PRIVATE REGISTERED PROVIDERS OF SOCIAL HOUSING: ASSURED PERIODIC TENANCY

In rent arrears claims, like local authorities, PRPSHs must comply with the Protocol dealt with at section 21 above.

Where the mandatory rent arrears ground is relied on, the landlord should comply with section 3 of the Protocol.

If after complying with the Protocol, a PRPSH still wishes to evict a tenant, it must serve a notice seeking possession. The notice is served under section 8 of the 1988 Act, and it must specify the ground on which possession is sought. The notice should also provide the particulars or details of the ground being relied on.

---

whether they are owed any duty under the homelessness legislation contained in part VII of the Housing Act 1996.

The court may dispense with the requirement to serve notice in relation to a discretionary ground. But it may only dispense with notice where it is just and equitable to do so.

The notice must also specify the date after which possession proceedings may be brought. The amount of notice that must be given varies according to which ground or grounds are relied on.

The amount of notice for each ground is as follows:

- Where ground 7A is relied on, either on its own or with other grounds, the date specified in the notice must not be earlier than the date on which a notice to quit would expire (see section 32 above).

- Where ground 14 is relied on, the date specified in the notice must be no earlier than the date the notice is served.

- The date specified in the notice must not be earlier than two months from the date the notice is served where:

    - grounds 1, 2, 5 to 7, 9 and 16 are relied on, either on their own or with other grounds; and

    - neither grounds 7A and 14 are being relied on.

Where any other grounds not mentioned above are relied on, the date specified in the notice must not be earlier than two weeks from the date the notice is served.

In some cases a landlord may be required to serve notice seeking possession on a non-tenant. This is where the ground or one of the grounds relied on is ground 14A.

Ground 14A applies where:

- The property was occupied by a couple.
- The couple are spouses, civil partners, or were living together as if they were spouses or civil partners.
- Either or both were tenants.
- One of them has left the property.
- They left because of violence or threats of violence from the other spouse, civil partner or equivalent partner.
- The violence or threats of violence were towards the partner who has left or a member of that partner's family who lived with them.
- And the court is satisfied that the partner who has left is unlikely to return.

In such a case, a PRPSH may rely on ground 14A to try to evict the partner still living at the property. If it does so, the landlord should also serve notice on the partner who left, even if they are a non-tenant. If the landlord cannot serve notice on the partner who left, it must at least have taken all reasonable steps to try to serve them.

The notice is valid for 12 months from the date it is served.

Section 8 of the 1988 Act refers to the notice being in the prescribed form. It does not expressly state using the prescribed form is a mandatory requirement. It's always the safest option to use the prescribed form, particularly when relying on mandatory grounds. But if, for instance, a landlord relying on a discretionary ground uses the wrong form, a court's power to dispense with service of the notice would allow it to dispense with service in this situation.

The court will require evidence that the notice has been served. This can be provided by a witness statement containing all relevant information. Or by completing the N215 form called a Certificate of Service. Such evidence is particularly important when relying on a mandatory ground because notice cannot be dispensed with.

35 – NOTICE REQUIRING POSSESSION SERVED BY A PRIVATE REGISTERED PROVIDERS OF SOCIAL HOUSING: FIXED-TERM TENANCY

Possession can only be recovered during the fixed-term of an assured tenancy where the wording of the agreement expressly allows this. This can be in the form of a contractual break clause or a forfeiture clause.

The break clause may only be relied on where any pre-conditions in the tenancy agreement for relying on the break clause are met. If the conditions are met, the landlord may serve notice seeking possession in accordance with the break clause.

When the notice expires, the fixed term is brought to an end, but a statutory periodic tenancy arises. Therefore, the landlord must obtain a court order for possession to end the statutory periodic tenancy that arises.

Forfeiture is rarely used by social landlords. In brief, it allows a landlord to re-enter the property where a tenant has breached the tenancy, the relevant demand for rent or notice of breach has been served, and has expired. Where there is a residential occupier, re-entry is effected by obtaining a forfeiture order from the court allowing re-entry. The occupier may apply to court for relief from forfeiture to suspend the landlord's re-entry.

Forfeiture can be complicated, so it is advisable to obtain specialist legal advice when bringing or defending forfeiture proceedings.

36 – ASSURED TENANCY GROUNDS FOR POSSESSION

When possession is sought from an assured tenant, only a ground or grounds contained at schedule 2 to the 1988 Act may be relied on. Schedule 2 contains a total of 22 grounds. These consist of discretionary grounds (ground 9 to 17), and mandatory grounds (grounds 1 to 8). The latter category includes an absolute ground for possession (ground 7A). The absolute ground applies where there has been a criminal conviction or proven anti-social behaviour. As with secure tenancies, rent arrears and anti-social behaviour are the grounds most commonly relied on to evict PRPSH tenants.

Schedule 2 to the 1988 Act contains 3 rent arrears grounds, one is mandatory (ground 8), and two are discretionary (grounds 10 and 11). It also contains 2 anti-social behaviour grounds, one is discretionary (ground 14), and the other is the absolute ground 7A.

The rent arrears grounds are set out below.

As it relates to tenants paying their rent weekly or monthly, ground 8 states:

> *Both at the date of service of the notice under section 8 of this Act relating to the proceedings for possession and at the date of the hearing-*
>
> *(a)* *if rent is payable weekly or fortnightly, at least eight weeks rent is unpaid;*
>
> *(b)* *if rent is payable monthly at least two months rent;*
>
> *(c)* ...

> *(d)* ...[6]
>
> *and for the purpose of this ground rent means rent lawfully due from the tenant.*

Ground 8 may only be relied on if at least the specified amount of arrears is owed **both** at the date notice is served **and** the date of the court hearing.

Ground 10 reads:

> *Some rent lawfully due from the tenant-*
>
> *(a)* *is unpaid on the date on which proceedings for possession are begun; and*
>
> *(b)* *except where subsection(1)(b) of section 8 of this Act applies*[7]*, was in arrears at the date of the service of the notice under that section relating to those proceedings.*

There are a number of differences between grounds 8 and 10. The most important difference is that ground 8 is mandatory. This means the court must make an outright possession order if ground 8 is proved. As ground 10 is discretionary, the court must also be satisfied it's reasonable to make a possession order, even when the ground is proved. The other differences are that with ground 10 there is no specified amount of rent that must be owed. So it can be relied on irrespective of the amount of arrears owed when notice is served, and when the claim is brought. But some arrears must be owed at both those dates, even if they are cleared before the court hearing.

---

6 Sub-paragraphs (c) and (d) deal respectively with rent payable quarterly and annually, which generally is not relevant to social housing tenancies.

7 Subsection 8(1)(b) deals with the court's power to dispense with service of the notice where it is just and equitable to do so.

However, if the court dispenses with notice under ground 10, it's only necessary for arrears to be owed when the claim is brought. In such a case the payment history may be particularly significant. The payment history could help the court to decide whether it's reasonable to make a possession order on a discretionary ground.

And ground 11 reads:

> *Whether or not any rent is in arrears on the date on which proceedings for possession are begun, the tenant has persistently delayed paying rent which has become lawfully due.*

A social landlord is only likely to rely on ground 11 if some rent is owed when the notice is served. But if the arrears are cleared before the possession claim is brought, the landlord may still continue with the claim. This is because ground 11 focuses on the tenant's past non-payment which resulted in the persistent failure to pay rent on time.

The discretionary anti-social behaviour ground available to PRPSHs is ground 14 at schedule 2 to the 1988 Act. It states:

The tenant or a person residing in or visiting the dwelling house-

> *(b)* *has been guilty of conduct causing or likely to cause a nuisance or annoyance to a person residing, visiting or otherwise engaging in lawful activity in the locality,*
>
> *(aa)* *has been guilty of conduct causing or likely to cause a nuisance or annoyance to the landlord of the dwelling house, or a person employed (whether or not by the landlord) in connection with the exercise of the landlord's housing management functions, and that is directly or indirectly related to or affects those functions, or*
>
> *(b)* *has been convicted of-*

(i) *using the dwelling-house or allowing it to be used for immoral or illegal purposes, or*

(ii) *an indictable offence committed in, or in the locality of the dwelling house.*

37 – USE BY PRIVATE REGISTERED PROVIDERS OF SOCIAL HOUSING OF THE ABSOULTE GROUND

Beyond inserting the new possession ground 7A, the HA 1988 contains limited additional provisions regarding the absolute ground. So unlike secure tenants, assured tenants do not have a statutory right to review their landlord's decision to rely on this ground.

However, some guidance is contained in the publication Anti-Social Behaviour Powers: Statutory Guidance for Frontline Professionals. It was first published by the Home Office in July 2014, and the most recent edition was updated in June 2022. The guidance applies to local authority and PRPSH landlords. It includes guidance on all aspects of the ASBCP Act 2014. It also provides guidance on using the absolute ground for possession. However, the section dealing with the absolute ground for possession indicates that section of the publication is non-statutory guidance.

The guidance sets out the expectations for PRPSHs seeking possession on the absolute ground. It expects PRPSHs to offer tenants an opportunity for a review of a decision to rely on this ground.

This guidance makes the non-statutory requirement for a review of claims under ground 7A of the 1988 Act, similar to statutory reviews applicable in claims under section 84A of the 1985 Act.

Social landlords are expected to comply with statutory guidance unless there are good reasons for not doing so. If they fail to do so without good reason, it may provide a tenant with a public law defence. However, guidance, even statutory guidance, is not legislation. And here the guidance regarding the absolute possession ground seems to be non-statutory guidance. In reality, social landlords generally have a procedure for carrying out such reviews.

38 – RECOVERING POSSESSION FROM AN ASSURED SHORTHOLD TENANT

An assured shorthold tenant has less security of tenure compared to an assured tenant. This is because the landlord does not have to prove a statutory ground to recover possession from an assured shorthold tenant.

Since publication of the RSH's Tenancy Standard, PRPSHs typically grant tenants an assured shorthold fixed-term tenancy for 5 years.

If a PRPSH wants to recover possession at the end of the fixed term, the notice requirements under sections 21(1A) and 21(1B) of the 1988 Act are as follows:

- The tenant must be given at least 6 months' written notice that the landlord does not intend to grant a further tenancy when the fixed term expires.
- The notice must advise the tenant of where they can obtain help or advice in relation to the notice.

The next step to recovering possession when relying on section 21 of the 1988 Act, is for the landlord to serve a notice requiring possession under section 21. A landlord must give at least two months' notice. However, the notice cannot be served in the first four months of the tenancy agreement.

The notice must be in the prescribed form, which is currently the Form 6A.

Possession proceedings must be brought within 6 months of the date the notice requiring possession was served.

Section 21 is effectively a mandatory possession claim. So, the landlord does not need to prove a statutory ground for possession, or that it's reasonable to make a possession order. However, if the reason the PRPSH seeks possession is due to rent arrears, Part 3 of the Protocol applies.

Although they are not statutorily required to do so, most PRPSH operate a review process when seeking possession under section 21. This provides tenants served with a section 21 notice the opportunity of a review of the decision to recover possession.

The PRPSH should have a policy setting out how any review procedure works, which procedure should be available to tenants served with a section 21 notice.

Even where a PRPSH grants an assured shorthold tenancy, some still rely on section 8 to recover possession. When the PRPSH does so, and relies on discretionary grounds the requirements set out at section 36 above apply, even though it is an assured shorthold tenancy.

39 – COMMON ISSUES WITH NOTICES

There are some differences in the requirements for serving notice under the 1985 and 1988 Acts. There are even differences within each Act depending on whether the ground is discretionary or mandatory. However, it's some common themes with these notices that is dealt with here.

One dispute that arises in relation to notices is whether the notice was in fact served on the tenant. It's for the landlord to prove notice was properly served. Therefore, formal written evidence from the individual who served the notice is advisable. That evidence can either be a certificate of service or a witness statement. It is also advisable for the person who served the notice to attend court at the possession hearing. The court can then hear evidence from them about service, if service is disputed.

A tenant who has not received the notice, and so wishes to challenge service may do so. But in some cases, it is not necessary for the court to be satisfied that the tenant actually received the notice. For instance, the tenancy may state notices sent by special delivery or first-class post will be treated as properly served. Where a tenancy agreement contains such a clause, the landlord only needs to prove that it has complied with that clause. Meaning there will be proper service if the landlord complies with the requirements in the tenancy agreement, even if the tenant does not receive the notice.

There are specific requirements about the date a notice must expire, and the contents of the notice. This may be raised as an issue if the information is incorrect. Courts normally take a pragmatic view, and assess whether there has been any disadvantage to the tenant. If there hasn't been, the court is more likely to dispense with service of the notice. Particularly if, despite any errors, it is reasonably clear who the intended recipient is, the property it relates to, and why possession is sought. Therefore, it's unlikely a typological error on its own, for instance, would be sufficient to challenge validity of the notice or to defend the claim.

CHAPTER FOUR

POSSESSION PROCEEDINGS

40 – AN OVERVIEW OF CLAIMS FOR POSSESSION

All litigation, particularly bringing a claim against a social tenant, should be a last resort. For instance, if the tenant is in arrears, the alternative options to proceedings contained in the Protocol should be explored first.

If there are allegations of anti-social behaviour, alternative ways of dealing with this should also be considered. That is especially so if the allegations are made against a tenant or other individual who is disabled or vulnerable. Alternative options to possession include mediation or obtaining an injunction. The alternative options can be found in the publication Anti-social behaviour powers: statutory guidance for frontline professionals.

Where possession proceedings are considered appropriate, it's for the landlord to prove that notice has been properly served. Or, if the discretionary ground is relied on, the landlord may persuade the court notice should be dispensed with. The landlord must also prove the ground, in other words, that there are rent arrears or there has been anti-social behaviour.

Even where the ground is proved, the court has a number of options available if a discretionary ground is relied on. The court may adjourn the claim, or possibly even dismiss the claim, although dismissing claims is less common.

The option landlords are generally looking for is that a possession order is made. Before the court makes a possession order it must be satisfied that it is reasonable to do so. And it must decide whether it is reasonable for the possession order to be outright or suspended. A fuller discussion of the rent arrears and anti-social behaviour grounds, reasonableness, and the different options available to the court is at sections 48 to 60 below.

Here, the court process for a landlord obtaining possession is summarised.

To begin court proceedings a landlord must apply to court after the relevant notice has expired. If the tenant vacates after the notice has expired, it's unlikely possession proceedings will be necessary. But if the tenant remains in occupation after expiry, proceedings must be brought to lawfully evict them. If the court makes a suspended possession order, that allows the tenant to remain in occupation, providing they comply with the terms of the order. If the court makes an outright possession order, that will require the tenant to vacate the property. In the latter case, if the tenant remains in the property beyond the date they are required to give up possession, the landlord must obtain a bailiff's warrant to enforce the possession order. The warrant will provide the tenant with the date on which the court bailiff will attend to evict them. The warrant gives the tenant at least 14 days' notice of the eviction date. But a tenant may also apply to suspend execution of the warrant. If that application is successful, it will stop the eviction going ahead.

41 – THE CIVIL PROCEDURE RULES

The procedure for bringing a claim is governed by the Civil Procedure Rules ("CPR"), and the accompanying Practice Directions ("CPR PD"). A comprehensive discussion of the CPR is beyond the scope of this book. Therefore, what follows relates to the parts of the CPR that are most relevant to possession claims.

The part that deals specifically with possession proceedings is CPR 55. This is sometimes referred to as part 55, and it covers the general rules.

CPR PD 55A supplements CPR 55, while CPR PD 55B deals with possession claims started online.

CPR 65 deals with demotion tenancies. But demotion tenancies are fairly uncommon, and so these are not dealt with in this book.

Virtually all possession claims are brought in the County Court. It's difficult to envisage a case where it would be appropriate to bring a possession claim for social housing in the High Court.

As part of the court process, each side has an opportunity to set out their case in writing. The landlord does so in the claim form and the particulars of claim. As the landlord brings the claim, the landlord is referred to as the claimant. The tenant's written case is set out in their defence. In possession proceedings, the tenant is known as the defendant.

The claim form, particulars of claim and defence are referred to as statements of case. Where one is brought, a written counterclaim is also a statement of case.

The claim can be made at any county court hearing centre by completing and submitting to court the relevant forms. The relevant forms are the claim form, which must be submitted with the particulars of claim. The claim form is on the N5 form; the information required to complete this form is explained on the form. It's normally advisable to use the court N119 Particulars of Claim form. The N119 form prompts the claimant to provide all necessary information, including any statutory grounds for possession. The N119A form contains guidance notes on completing the N119. But a claimant may prepare their own particulars of claim instead, setting out the basis of the claim.

When starting the claim, additional relevant documents can be submitted at the same time as the claim form and particulars of claim.

The following additional relevant documents are sometimes submitted with the claim form and particulars of claim when starting the claim:

- The signed tenancy agreement;
- The notice seeking possession;
- Evidence dealing with service of the notice (either a witness statement or Certificate of Service).

There may be other documents that would be useful in a particular case. For example, in anti-social behaviour cases, providing a schedule of the allegations relied on can be useful.

Sufficient copies of the forms need to be provided to the court when submitting the claim. This means a copy for each party, including one for each joint tenant if it's a joint tenancy. A copy for the court to retain on the court file must also be provided. The hearing centre will issue the claim, assign a claim number which is the reference number for the proceedings. Each side should include the claim number in any communications with the court. The court will send a "Notice of Issue" to the claimant which provides the date the claim was issued and the allocated claim number.

On issuing the claim, the hearing centre will also set a date and time for the first possession hearing. It will enter these details on the claim form, and provide the claimant with details regarding the hearing.

The claim form and particulars of claim will be sent to the defendant(s). Typically, the hearing date must be at least 21 days from the date the claim form and particulars of claim are served on the defendant. But the court has the power to shorten the period between starting a claim and the date for the first hearing in certain cases. CPR PD 55 expressly refers to appropriate cases where this power may be used. Those include cases where the landlord's employee or a local resident has been threatened or assaulted by the tenant or a member of their household.

As stated, the claim can be made at any hearing centre. If the hearing centre does not serve the address where the property is situated, it will still issue the claim. Afterwards it will transfer the claim to the hearing centre serving the area the property is located in. The hearing centre the claim has been transferred to will set the date and time for the hearing. It will then send the claim form containing that information, and the particulars of claim, to the defendant.

When sending out the claim form and particulars of claim, the defendant will also be sent a N11R form. This is a proforma defence form. It's mainly designed for rent arrears cases, and even has limited space to include brief information about counterclaims. There is more information about counterclaims below. The defendant will also receive a N7A form providing some information about what to do next.

If possible, a defendant who wishes to defend the claim should try to obtain legal advice from a housing specialist. This can be obtained from housing solicitors or other organisation (such as a law centre). In some cases, public funding (i.e. legal aid) may cover the cost of this advice. Firms and organisations carrying out legally aided housing work can assess an individual's eligibility for public funding.

To defend the claim, a defendant should complete the N11R defence form. Or they could prepare an individualised written defence in response to the claim. In whatever format the defence is prepared, it should address separately each aspect of the claim that is disputed. It should also make clear which, if any, aspects of the claim are accepted. CPR 15 and 16 deal with defences.

A signed copy of the defence should be sent to the court and the claimant. Ideally this should be done within 14 days of receiving the particulars of claim. If that's not possible, every effort should be made to send the defence out before the first court hearing date. If legal advice has been obtained, the legal adviser may assist with or prepare the defence on the defendant's behalf.

All statements of case and witness statements that are submitted must be signed and include a statement of truth. An electronic signature is acceptable. The wording of a statement of truth is at CPR PD 22.

42 – POSSESSION CLAIMS ONLINE

Where a possession claim is brought due to rent arrears, the claim may be started online. The online system is referred to as possession claims online or PCOL. The procedure must not be used to claim any remedy other than the payment of rent arrears.

The landlord must complete the claim form online. The particulars of claim must be submitted with the claim form. The relevant fee should also be paid electronically.

The landlord should provide a rent statement for the last two years. Or a rent statement going back to when the account was last in credit, if that was than less than two years ago. The rent statement could be provided with the online claim form.

Alternatively, if the schedule was provided to the tenant before the claim was started, the landlord need only submit a summary of the arrears with the claim form. If the landlord does so, the full rent schedule must be sent to the tenant within 7 days of the claim being issued. The landlord must provide oral evidence, or written evidence in a witness statement, confirming these requirements have been complied with.

When the claim is issued, the court will send a printed copy of the claim form and the defence form to the tenant. It will also send the landlord a notice of issue.

The defendant may submit their defence or defence and counterclaim online or in written form.

All statements of case and witness statements must be signed and include a statement of truth. An electronic signature is acceptable. The wording of a statement of truth is at CPR PD 22.

43 – ACCELERATED POSSESSION PROCEEDINGS

Like private sector landlords, PRPSHs may use the accelerated possession procedure to recover possession. But it can only be used in certain cases.

CPR 55.11 and CPR 55.12 set out in full all the circumstances that must apply where the accelerated procedure is used.

The following are amongst the conditions which must be satisfied if the accelerated possession procedure is used:

- The property is let under an assured shorthold tenancy.
- Proceedings have been initiated by a notice served under section 21 of the 1988 Act.
- The tenancy began after 28th February 1997.
- The only purpose of the claim is to obtain possession of the property.
- And the tenancy or tenancies are all written agreements.

An accelerated claim is started by submitting the N5B claim form with all sections completed.

The court will serve the claim form on the defendant, normally by first class post.

A defendant who wishes to defend the claim must file a defence within 14 days of receiving the claim form. Filing a document means submitting a copy of the document to the court. They should use the N11B form. This form can also be used if the defendant agrees to the order but wants longer than 14 days to vacate. If the defendant completes the N11B form, the court will send a copy to the claimant.

If the claimant doesn't receive a defence, they can make a written request for a possession order to be granted. That request will be referred to a judge.

If a defence is sent to the court, the claim form and defence are referred to a judge.

The judge will consider the claim form, and any defence, if one has been submitted. The judge will then decide whether to make a possession order. If so, this may be done without a hearing.

Alternatively, the claim will be listed for a hearing if the judge isn't satisfied the landlord is entitled to possession. The case may also be listed for a hearing if the defendant requests longer than the standard 14 days to vacate the property. The judge may also strike out the claim if it has no reasonable prospect of success.

If the matter is dealt with without a hearing, an application may be made to set-aside the order. Any such application must be made within 14 days of receiving the order. The application can be made in relation to an order for possession or one striking out the claim.

44 – COURT HEARING

The objective of bringing a claim is for the court to resolve a dispute between the parties which they cannot resolve between themselves.

When a possession claim is brought to court, the court can deal with it in the following ways:

- By making a possession order, which can be an outright or suspended possession order.
- By adjourning the claim to a date for a further hearing to be held.
- By adjourning the claim generally, where no new court date is planned.
- Or by dismissing the claim altogether.

These options are dealt with below. Examples in this section relate to arrears' claims, but the information also applies to claims brought on other grounds.

In some cases, the claim is resolved (or disposed of) by having a contested trial. At a trial the court hears evidence and legal arguments from both sides (i.e. the parties). The court then reaches a decision about the case based on the facts, the law and the evidence. Sometimes after a claim starts, the parties reach an agreement between themselves about how to deal with the dispute. This is referred to as settling the claim.

The first court hearing is usually on a busy court list with many other cases. This means it's likely to be allocated limited court time, possibly just 5 to 10 minutes. This makes it impractical for the court to carry out a detailed examination of each sides' case at the first hearing.

At the first possession hearing, the court could dispose of the claim by making a possession order. This could be an outright or suspended possession order. If an outright possession order is made on a mandatory ground, this should be made clear in the order. This is because whether the order is made on the mandatory or discretionary grounds will affect the options available to a defendant after the possession order is made. Possession orders are dealt with in more detail in section 46 below.

The court could dispose of the claim by dismissing it. This is fairly unusual if there were arrears at the date the notice was served and/or the claim was issued. Even if any previous arrears have been cleared by the date of the hearing. In this situation the court may adjourn the claim generally (see below) instead of dismissing it. A claim is only likely to be dismissed if there is something fundamentally wrong with the claim or the way it's been brought. Even then, most errors could probably be corrected without dismissing the claim.

45 – ADJOURNMENTS

At the first hearing the court may adjourn the claim. It may also adjourn the claim at a subsequent hearing. This would be appropriate where the defendant genuinely disputes the claim on grounds which appear to be substantial. This can normally be identified from any defence that has been filed and served. This is why it is important for a defendant who contests the claim to prepare their defence before the hearing. Any adjournment on this basis is likely to be with case management directions. Such directions provide a timetable for dealing with the procedural steps required to progress the claim. Typical directions include dates by which each side must disclose documents to the other side, and dates by which they must prepare witness statements. This is done in preparation for a future trial. Although further interim hearings may be necessary before the trial takes place.

Alternatively, a claim may be adjourned to give one or more parties the opportunity to take some relevant action. The action could be to provide more information which would help the court dispose of the claim at a subsequent hearing. More information may help the court decide how to deal with a case even if the defendant accepts the arrears are owed. These could be issues relevant to whether it's reasonable to make a possession order, or what type of possession order. For example, if a claim for welfare benefits or a Discretionary Housing Payment has been made but not yet decided. The court may want to see if that application reduces the arrears before deciding how to deal with the claim. Or the court may want more information about the health or other support needs of the defendant or a household member.

As with defended claims described above, where the court adjourns cases to get more information, the court should give instructions on what steps need to be taken. The instructions (sometimes called directions) should explain what needs to be done, which party will do it, and the timescale for doing it. The court normally also deals with when the next hearing will take place, and the time estimate for the next hearing. Dealing with when the claim will next be heard can be done in one of two ways. Firstly, by providing the parties with the time and date of the next hearing. Or secondly, by indicating the earliest time frame the matter will return to court for a hearing. In the second situation the claim will be listed on the first available court date after that time frame. For example, the court may say there will be a further hearing on the first available date after 14 days. The actual date will be confirmed in writing by the court later.

A different type of adjournment is where the claim is adjourned generally. An adjournment generally is similar to disposing of the claim. However, it allows the case to be easily returned to court if necessary. This might happen where the court has all the necessary information, and decides it's unreasonable to make a possession order. For example, after all benefit claims have been exhausted, a defendant may have a modest amount of arrears. If the arrears are low, the court may consider an order, even a suspended possession order, is unreasonable. But it may also be inappropriate to dismiss the claim.

In such cases, adjourning the claim generally could be the appropriate option. It would be adjourned on condition that the defendant repays the arrears by instalments. No date will be set for a further hearing, but there will normally be a cut-off date. Before the cut-off date, the parties can apply for the case to be listed for a hearing. So where a claim is adjourned generally, the landlord may request a court hearing if the defendant fails to make the required payments. Or the defendant may request a hearing if they want to reduce the amount of the instalments. If neither party requests a further hearing before the cut-off date, the case will be dismissed.

46 – POSSESSION ORDERS

The alternative to adjourning or dismissing the claim is a possession order. There are two types of possession orders. Firstly, an outright possession order, which requires the defendant to leave the property by a specified date. In other words, this is an eviction order. Secondly, the court can make a suspended possession order. This also requires the defendant to leave their home. However, the requirement to leave is suspended so long as they comply with conditions specified in the order.

The court's power to make a possession order is contained in section 84 of the 1985 Act, and section 7 of the 1988 Act.

Before making a possession order, there are certain procedural and substantive matters the court needs to be satisfied about. The court will need evidence from the landlord on these matters. Some landlords submit this evidence at the same time as submitting the claim form and particulars of claim. If that hasn't been done, it should be provided at least two days before the hearing. Copies should be sent to both the tenant and to court.

Firstly, the court needs evidence about the tenancy. Providing the court with a copy of the signed tenancy agreement is normally sufficient.

Secondly, the court requires evidence regarding the notice seeking possession. Again, the court will want to see a copy of the notice. This will whether:

- It is in the appropriate format;
- Contains the relevant information (i.e. the statutory ground and particulars);
- Gave the tenant adequate notice;
- The notice period had expired before proceedings were issued; and
- The proceedings were issued while the notice was valid (e.g. within 6 months of service of a section 21 notice, and within 12 months for most other notices).

Thirdly, the court requires evidence that the notice seeking possession was served on the tenant. This is normally provided by either a witness statement or certificate of service signed by the person who served it. Alternatively, the court can hear oral evidence from the landlord's representative about when and how the notice was served. It is advisable for the individual who served the notice to attend court in case the tenant disputes receiving it. That means the person who served the notice can give direct evidence about this to the court if there is a dispute.

Finally, to prove the ground for possession, the court requires information regarding the arrears. This should be a rent statement going back two years. Although a shorter period would be acceptable if the account was in credit in the last two years. In which case, a statement going back to when it was last in credit is sufficient. But a landlord may provide a statement going further back if they are relying on a long poor payment history. Where the current rent on is different to the rent on the tenancy agreement, it's advisable to have evidence about this. Letters sent to the tenant notifying them of variations to the rent should be sufficient.

Next, in discretionary claims, the court needs to consider whether it's reasonable to make a possession order. And if so, what type of possession order to make.

47 – REASONABLENESS IN RENT ARREARS CLAIMS

The court has a wide discretion on whether it is reasonable to make a possession order on a discretionary ground. The discretion is contained in sections 84 and 85 of the 1985 Act, and sections 7 and 9 of the 1988 Act.

Because it's a wide discretion, this makes it difficult to list all the factors the court may take into account. However, some common considerations are:

- the reason for the arrears;
- the amount of arrears;
- how long arrears have been owed and the tenant's general payment history;
- what advice or assistance the social landlord has offered, and whether the tenant has engaged with the help offered;
- the future likelihood of the tenant paying the rent when it's due, plus repaying the arrears by reasonable instalments; and
- whether the landlord has complied with the pre-action protocol and any policy it has regarding rent arrears.

Wider factors beyond the rent and arrears may also be relevant to how the court exercises its discretion. For instance, the court may consider the likely effect of eviction on any household member. This can be especially relevant where an eviction is likely to have a particularly negative effect on a household member. That could be because of a medical condition. The effect of an eviction on any children could also be relevant. For instance, where a child has additional learning support needs. Particularly if an eviction could put them at risk of having to change school.

A social landlord will also have arguments on why it's reasonable for the court to make the order it's seeking. For instance, it may argue that affordable social housing is scarce. That means there are many applicants on the waiting list for social housing who would pay their rent. It may also argue it relies on rent payments to provide, maintain and repair its social housing.

There is potentially an endless list of factors that may be relevant to reasonableness. It's the judge's role to weigh up the different factors, and decide what is the most appropriate decision to make.

Therefore, a social landlord who wants to evict a tenant needs to satisfy the court of a number of things. Firstly, it must prove the ground for possession. Secondly, that it is reasonable to make a possession order. And thirdly, that it is reasonable to make an outright possession order.

If the court makes an outright order on a discretionary ground, it has a broad discretion to decide on the date the tenant must vacate the property. But if possession is on a mandatory ground, the date for possession should be up to 14 days from the date the order is made. The court may only allow a longer period if vacating in 14 days would cause exceptional hardship. Exceptional hardship needs to be more than the tenant becoming homeless because that is not considered exceptional when possession orders are made. But in any event, the maximum period the court can allow in mandatory claims is 42 days.

As stated, if a suspended possession order is made, the tenant can remain in occupation providing they comply with the conditions imposed by the order.

Landlords usually request a money judgment order in rent arrears claims. And if the court makes an outright or suspended possession order, it will also make a money judgment order.

The money judgment order is an order stating the amount owed to the landlord. This will include the amount of rent arrears owed at the date the order is made. It will also include costs if an order for costs is made.

Where a suspended possession order is made in rent arrears cases, it will be suspended on condition that the arrears are repaid by instalments. The money judgment order will also be repaid in instalments. The amount of the instalments must be reasonable (i.e. affordable). Where a tenant is dependent on welfare benefits, a common practice is to limit instalments to 5% of their standard allowance. Depending on the amount of arrears owed, it may take many years to repay the arrears. For social housing tenants, that situation is not unusual. Ultimately, it's for the judge to decide on the instalments and whether that would mean the arrears are repaid within a reasonable period.

48 – COSTS

The general rule is that a successful party is entitled to their costs of pursuing a claim.

If the landlord obtains a possession order it is normally entitled to costs. If no defence has been submitted, the landlord is entitled to fixed costs only. This is a standard (or fixed) amount set out at CPR 45.5.

Fixed costs don't apply if the landlord obtains a possession order after a defence has been submitted. In that case, the landlord could claim an amount greater than the fixed costs level, particularly if it has been legally represented. The landlord's legal costs may include court fees paid as well as the cost of legal representation.

There is normally costs protection for a tenant who is legally aided. Costs protection applies from the date legal aid is granted. It protects the tenant by suspending the requirement to pay the landlord's costs for as long as they are on a low income. Therefore, if the court orders they must pay their landlord's costs, the costs order cannot be enforced without an assessment of the tenant's ability to pay them.

49 – COMMON POSSESSION CLAIM SCENARIO

Each case is different, and a variety of outcomes are described above. However, some scenarios are more common than others. For instance, although the first hearing is normally a short hearing, if the landlord's case has been properly prepared, the court could dispose of the case at the first hearing.

This may happen if the tenant agrees with what the landlord says about the case, and agrees with what the landlord's asking for. This is also more likely to happen if the tenant does not attend the court hearing. Tenants not attending is a relatively typical scenario. For instance, if the landlord's representative intends to ask the court to make a suspended possession order. Sometimes the landlord's representative may advise the tenant that there is no need for them to attend the hearing. Because a suspended possession order allows the tenant to carry on living in their home. A tenant who is stressed about attending court may welcome the chance not to attend, particularly if they can carry on living in their home. However, it is normally advisable for tenants to attend the hearing, particularly because they can usually see the duty adviser at court.

50 – DUTY ADVISER

On days when the court is dealing with possession claims, there may be a duty adviser available. The duty adviser will provide specialist housing advice to unrepresented tenants at court. Duty advisers can also represent a tenant during the court hearing. They will write to the tenant after the hearing to explain what happened at court. But a duty adviser will not provide ongoing representation. This will only happen if they later enter into a separate agreement with the tenant to do so.

51 – KEY POINTS IN RENT ARREARS CLAIMS

Some key points in rent arrears claims are set out below.

Ground 8 of schedule 2 to the 1988 Act is the only mandatory rent arrears ground available in respect of an assured tenancy. The court requires strict compliance with relevant procedure before it will consider making a possession order on this ground. For example, it cannot dispense with the requirement to serve notice seeking possession. But if the landlord shows it is entitled to rely on ground 8, the court must normally make an outright possession order. Therefore, if the correct procedure has been followed, and the relevant amount of arrears were owed at the appropriate stages, an outright possession order will be made. There are only limited exceptions to this, for instance, if a counterclaim or a public law defence is available. These are dealt with below.

In all arrears' cases, a claim may only be made for rent that is lawfully due from the tenant. This is irrespective of whether the claim is under the 1985 or 1988 Acts, or a mandatory or discretionary ground. This is relevant where a tenant also has a claim against their landlord. Because a tenant entitled to compensation from their landlord, is entitled to set-off that compensation against the arrears. This means the value of the tenant's set-off must be deducted from the arrears to calculate the amount of rent lawfully due from the tenant.

Here a "set-off" refers to any cross-claim the tenant may have, which would entitle the tenant to compensation. So a tenant would have to bring their own cross-claim (known as a counterclaim) against the landlord within the possession proceedings. Therefore, any compensation (often called damages) awarded to the tenant will be deducted from the arrears owed to the landlord.

This means counterclaims can be particularly important in claims where the mandatory rent arrears ground is relied. Because if damages awarded for the counterclaim eliminate the arrears, the mandatory ground is no longer available. Or, if damages for the counterclaim reduce the arrears below eight weeks or two months, again, the mandatory ground cannot be relied on.

52 – DISREPAIR COUNTERCLAIMS

Disrepair and other poor housing conditions are the most common counterclaims brought by tenants. This counterclaim is available where the landlord is responsible for repairs or works to the property which it has failed to carry out.

Tenants are strongly advised not to withhold rent payments because of poor conditions. But if they fall into rent arrears, these conditions may provide a defence or a partial defence, as well as being a counterclaim.

As such, the written counterclaim should be submitted at the same time as the defence. The defence and counterclaim should also be contained in the same document. If they are submitted at the same time, the tenant will not need the court's permission to bring the counterclaim. But if the counterclaim is brought after the defence has been submitted, the court's permission will be required. The court will normally want to see a copy of the proposed counterclaim before giving permission.

The tenant may have to pay a court fee for bringing the counterclaim.

It should also be remembered a tenant may bring a counterclaim at any time before a possession order is executed. So a tenant may bring a counterclaim when applying to suspend a warrant (see below), even if it wasn't brought earlier in the proceedings.

Disrepair and poor housing conditions can be legally complex. Therefore, a detailed analysis is beyond the scope of this book. Where housing conditions becomes an issue in possession claims, it's advisable to seek specialist advice.

In summary, a landlord is responsible for carrying out certain works or repairs. A social landlord's responsibility will normally be set out in the written tenancy agreement. The law also requires landlords carry out certain works or repairs, irrespective of what is contained in the tenancy agreement. In other words, the tenancy agreement cannot override the repairs a landlord is required to carry out by law. A social landlord may agree to carry out more repairs or works than it's statutorily required to. In which case, the failure to carry out those additional repairs or works stated in the tenancy can also be relied on by the tenant.

The law is contained in sections 9A and 11 of the Landlord and Tenant Act 1985.

Section 9A of the Landlord and Tenant Act 1985 is an amendment introduced in recent years. It applies to all tenancies granted by social landlords after it came into force on 20th March 2019. However, different rules apply to tenancies that already existed at that date. These rules are set out at section 9B of the Landlord and Tenant Act 1985. So reference should be made to section 9B to determine whether or from when the provisions apply to these earlier tenancies.

Section 9A requires property let under a tenancy is fit for human habitation at the date it is let, and throughout the tenancy. The term fit for human habitation is defined at section 10 of the Landlord and Tenant Act 1985.

By section 11 of the Landlord and Tenant Act 1985, landlords are responsible for repairing the structure and exterior of a property. They are also responsible for repairing the heating, hot water, and installations that supply gas, electricity, water, and that provide sanitation.

If a landlord breaches sections 9A or 11, a tenant could claim compensation or damages. To do so, the landlord must first have knowledge that works or repairs are needed. The landlord is also allowed a reasonable period to carry out the repair or works before they are liable to pay damages. If they fail to do so, these are the damages which a tenant can set-off against rent arrears.

53 – DISCRIMINATION COUNTERCLAIMS

Counterclaims alleging a landlord has discriminated against the tenant, are also becoming more common. In most cases, the counterclaim is based on allegations of discrimination due to a person's disability.

Discrimination and other types of related claims are governed by the Equality Act 2010. The types of counterclaims and defences available to tenants under the Equality Act are dealt with below.

54 – ANTI-SOCIAL BEHAVIOUR CLAIMS

Applying for a possession order is one of a number of tools available to social landlords to deal with anti-social behaviour. Possession is considered one of the last resorts, therefore landlords should consider whether there may be other methods of dealing with the anti-social behaviour.

The frontline guidance sets out some of the other tools, such as mediation or injunctions. The frontline guidance also deals with possession on the absolute ground.

Where a possession claim is brought due to anti-social behaviour, the claim is more likely to be disposed of at a fully contested trial when compared to rent arrears claims. This is because there are more likely to be factual disputes in anti-social behaviour cases. The dispute may be around whether the alleged behaviour has taken place. And if the behaviour is proved, disputes may arise about who has committed the anti-social behaviour.

55 – KEY ISSUES IN ANTI-SOCIAL BEHAVIOUR CASES

Anti-social behaviour covers a wide spectrum of behaviour. This can range from low level nuisance behaviour, to serious and sustained criminal activity. In serious cases, if the relevant criteria is met, a social landlord is more likely to rely on the absolute ground for possession.

The discretionary anti-social behaviour at ground 2 under the 1985 Act is identical to the discretionary anti-social behaviour at ground 14 under the 1988 Act (see sections 23 and 36 above).

Most social housing tenancy agreements will include a term making the tenant responsible for their own behaviour, and responsible for the behaviour of anyone else residing in or visiting their property. That breadth is reflected in the wording of discretionary anti-social behaviour statutory grounds (see sections 23 and 36 above). In other words, this ground can be made out even if the tenant's behaviour is blameless, but a household member or visitor behaves anti-socially.

There are two aspects of anti-social behaviour to which the discretionary ground applies. The first aspect covers nuisance and annoyance behaviour, the second applies where there is a conviction for immoral, illegal and criminal behaviour. There can be some overlap because criminal activity may also cause a nuisance and annoyance to others.

The first aspect of the discretionary ground relating to nuisance and annoyance refers to the individual being "guilty of conduct". But this aspect of the ground is available even if there is no conviction or judicial finding that the behaviour has taken place.

Behaviour which actually causes a nuisance or annoyance is covered, but so too is behaviour that is likely to cause a nuisance or annoyance. So this ground may be relied on even without direct evidence the behaviour has actually caused a nuisance.

It is also capable of covering low-level behaviour, such as behaviour that is likely to cause an annoyance. However, it seems unlikely a social landlord would bring a claim for an isolated incident of low-level annoyance, such as a garden that is briefly unkempt. Or if it did, the court is unlikely to find it reasonable to make a possession order.

The individuals protected by this ground are also broad: it covers other tenants, their households, their visitors, and effectively anyone who is engaged in lawful activity in the locality of the property. It also covers those working on behalf of the landlord, whether those individuals are in the locality or not.

The second aspect of the discretionary ground is based on whether the tenant, household member or a visitor to the property has been convicted of using or allowing the property to be used for immoral or illegal purposes. Or if the tenant, resident or visitor has been convicted of an indictable offence. An indictable offence excludes offences that can only be tried in the magistrates' court.

The wording of the discretionary ground means a low level non-indictable conviction may be sufficient if the property was used for the purposes of committing the offence. But the ground does not cover low level crimes where the property was not used to commit the offence. For instance, it would not cover a minor road traffic offence. Whereas a conviction for a more serious, indictable offence, unconnected to the property, but committed within the locality is covered. An indictable offence that took place before the tenancy began may also be relied on.

There is no precise definition of "locality", but it is almost certainly likely to apply to the building, road or street a property is situated in. It's also likely to apply to adjacent roads, and an estate if that is where the property is situated. It could also arguably apply to the entire local authority area in which a property is situated. In some cases, whether behaviour has taken place in the locality of a property may be a point of dispute that the court will have to decide on.

Where a landlord seeks possession on the discretionary anti-social behaviour ground, there a number of possible defences. Firstly, the tenant may argue the conduct did not take place.

Secondly the tenant may dispute who is responsible for the behaviour complained of. They may argue that the person responsible is not the tenant, a resident or visitor. This defence may be established or undermined by visual and/or audio recordings. Such recordings are increasingly a feature of evidence relied on in these types of cases.

In some cases, social landlords may need to decide whether the appropriate response is sanctions or safeguarding. For instance, where neighbours complain about hearing domestic arguments or fighting, domestic abuse may be relevant. Or where there is criminal activity associated with a property, this may be due to a vulnerable tenant being exploited. Social landlords should have safeguarding policies, and it may be these rather than, or in addition, to anti-social behaviour policies, that need to be followed.

As the threshold of behaviour likely to cause a nuisance or annoyance is low, arguably a social landlord could apply for a possession order for an isolated incident of minor problematic behaviour. In reality, most social landlords are likely to address this situation by exploring alternatives to possession proceedings in the first instance. This is a sensible approach for a number of reasons. Firstly, social landlords will have a policy and procedure for dealing with anti-social behaviour, and these policies normally recommend using tools such as warning letters, mediation, and/or acceptable behaviour agreements for low-level conduct. Secondly, bringing possession proceedings uses financial and personnel resources, which is likely to be a disproportionate response. Finally, the court may conclude it is not reasonable to make a possession order in this situation, even if the allegations are made out.

Another consequence of the low threshold is tenants have limited opportunity to successfully arguing that the alleged behaviour doesn't satisfy the anti-social behaviour ground.

56 – THE EQUALITY ACT IN ANTI-SOCIAL BEHAVIOUR CLAIMS

The Equality Act 2010 may be relevant in anti-social behaviour cases. It may be relevant where someone is subjected to anti-social behaviour due to their protected characteristic. Or if someone's protected characteristic, such as a disability, has caused or contributed to them behaving anti-socially.

A protected characteristic refers to the characteristics an individual has which are protected by the Equality Act. Disability is the protected characteristic most frequently raised in these cases, particularly being raised as a defence. But other protected characteristics may also be relevant.

The Equality Act 2010 is discussed in more detail at section 59 below.

57 – REASONABLENESS IN ANTI-SOCIAL BEHAVIOUR CLAIMS

Anti-social behaviour is a complex social issue, which may involve social landlords working with various organisations when trying to address it. For instance, working with the police, social services and other support agencies such as Victim Support, drug and alcohol support services, and mental health teams.

There is increasing emphasis on considering the effect of anti-social behaviour on neighbours and communities. And social landlords will want to support those affected by the anti-social behaviour of others.

This emphasis led to the insertion of section 85A into the 1985 Act, and section 9A being inserted into the 1988 Act.

These provisions set out factors relevant to whether it's reasonable to make a possession order on discretionary anti-social behaviour grounds. The court must consider these factors when dealing with claims brought on these grounds. The factors are:

- The effect the anti-social behaviour has had on others;
- The continuing effects the anti-social behaviour is likely to have on others; and
- The effect the behaviour would be likely to have on others if it's repeated.

In some cases, taking these factors into account may need to be balanced with supporting tenants whose properties are the source of anti-social behaviour. For instance, mental health problems, substance misuse and/or exploitation by others may be causing or contributing to such behaviour.

In addition to the statutory factors relevant to reasonableness, many others may also be relevant, as set out below.

If someone other than the tenant is responsible for the anti-social behaviour, that may be relevant to reasonableness. Particularly if the person responsible is a visitor and not a household member. And especially if the tenant can ensure they will no longer visit the property. However, that may be insufficient to persuade the court a possession order is unreasonable. Particularly if the anti-social behaviour has been serious and/or prolonged.

The type of anti-social behaviour will be relevant. For instance, the supply of drugs within the locality, is likely to justify an outright possession order being made. But less serious conduct over a sustained period may also be sufficient, such as noise nuisance. Especially if neighbours provide evidence regarding the effects on them of the noise nuisance.

Violence and threats towards the landlord's employees and/or contractors are regarded as extremely serious.

It may be less clear-cut where complaints are made about a person's so-called aggressive behaviour. In some circumstances, social landlords may need to ensure there is no unconscious racial bias influencing how someone's behaviour is perceived.

Some of the arguments relied on as public law defences may also be raised as defences to discretionary anti-social behaviour claims. In particular, where a social landlord has failed to follow its anti-social behaviour policy.

The main public law defences relied on in possession proceedings are discussed below.

58 – PUBLIC LAW DEFENCES

So far, when considering issues relating to recovering possession, these have been based on the parties' private law rights. For instance, the landlord's ownership rights to the rented accommodation. The landlord's right to bring a possession claim where a statutory ground is made out has also been considered. The reasons for bringing the claim have been based on the expected behaviour of tenants. This may be contractual when it's based on the express wording of the tenancy agreement. So for instance, the tenants' obligation to pay the rent, and not to behave anti-socially.

There is an additional category of defences known as public law defences. Public law defences can be particularly relevant where a social housing tenant has limited or no security of tenure. Because these defences can be relied on in claims brought on mandatory or absolute grounds. Or in claims against introductory and assured shorthold tenants. They can also be relevant where the court must be satisfied about whether it's reasonable to make a possession order. But there is often considerable overlap between the requirements of public law and reasonableness.

Defences described as public law defences ordinarily cannot be brought against a private landlord. There is one exception, which is discrimination claims: it is unlawful for both private and social landlords to discriminate. But the other public law defences are only available to social housing tenants, including where the Equality Act public sector equality duty has been breached.

Therefore, where public law defences are available, they can be used in claims brought by local authorities. They can also be used against PRPSHs. But they can only be relied on against PRPSHs if the PRPSH is acting in a public capacity. So for instance, where a tenant has been allocated affordable rented accommodation through the local authority's housing register (i.e. waiting list). If the accommodation is owned by a PRPSH, the PRPSH is likely to be acting in a public capacity.

But PRPSHs sometimes also act in a private or commercial capacity. For instance, where the PRPSH charges its tenants a market rent.

In addition to rent levels, other factors may help determine whether a PRPSH is acting in a private or public capacity.

Firstly, how the PRPSH acquired the property. For instance, whether it's previously owned local authority housing stock transferred from the local authority. Or whether the PRPSH has renovated, built or purchased the accommodation using privately raised funds.

Secondly, the terms of the tenancy agreement may be another indicator. For instance, where the tenancy agreement allows a mutual exchange, that is consistent with social housing. Therefore, the landlord is likely to be treated as acting in a public capacity.

Public law defences are based on the fact that social landlords are carrying out a public function by providing social housing. Therefore, they are expected to act in a way that is consistent with that social objective.

There are many categories of public law defences, but these can be broken down in to five main groups. This defence may be available where a social landlord has acted in the following ways:

- Illegally;
- Irrationally;
- In a procedurally irregular manner;
- Breaching the Equality Act 2010; or
- Breaching article 8 of the European Convention on Human Rights ("ECHR").

Illegality refers to cases where a social landlord acts outside its lawful authority. For instance, a local authority that grants introductory tenancies to new tenants. That would be unlawful if the local authority's executive has not elected to operate such a scheme.

Irrationality is equivalent to acting in a perverse or absurd manner. Where this is relied on, it normally relates to the way a social landlord has used its discretionary powers. In reality the court rarely makes a finding of irrationality because it is a hard test to satisfy. Irrationality is a much higher test than simply disagreeing with the way a social landlord has acted.

Irrationally means no right-minded social landlord, even one presented with the same information, would have acted in the same way. An example may be where a tenant is dependent on housing benefit to pay their rent. They make a prompt application for housing benefit to the local authority providing all the information needed to process the claim. This is followed by an unjustified delay in the local authority processing the claim. The delay causes the tenant to fall into rent arrears. The housing benefit claim is eventually processed and eliminates all the arrears. If the same local authority brought a possession claim due to the now-cleared rent arrears, that would be irrational.

Procedural irregularity is sometimes referred to as procedural unfairness or procedural impropriety. It covers a variety of situations where public authorities have adopted an unfair process, including the following:

- Denying individuals affected by decisions the opportunity to raise points or provide evidence before the decision is reached.
- Failing to consider relevant arguments and evidence presented.
- Taking irrelevant matters into account.
- A public authority failing to comply with its own policies.

- A decision maker providing inadequate reasons for an adverse decision.

Whether a public authority has acted fairly will depend on the facts of each individual case. For instance, a public authority may not consider a household member's medical condition when deciding whether to pursue an eviction. Ordinarily, that would amount to procedural unfairness. But under different circumstances this may not be procedurally unfair. For instance, if the public authority has not been informed about the medical condition. And there was no reason why the public authority ought to have known about the medical condition.

59 – EQUALITY ACT 2010

Tenants may rely on the Equality Act 2010. For instance, if a landlord has discriminated against them, this could provide a defence. They may also be entitled to damages, so could bring a counterclaim as well. A defence may also be available where a social landlord has breached its public sector equality duty. But as damages cannot be claimed where a landlord breaches this duty, this would not provide a counterclaim.

In very broad terms, the objective of the Equality Act is to promote equality and eliminate discrimination and other prohibited conduct. This behaviour is unlawful where it is due to a person's protected characteristic.

The protected characteristics under the Equality Act are:

- Age
- Disability
- Gender reassignment

- Marriage and civil partnership
- Race
- Religion or belief
- Sex
- Sexual orientation
- Pregnancy and maternity

Direct and Indirect Discrimination

Discrimination can be in the form of direct or indirect discrimination. And the Equality Act expressly prohibits discrimination in relation to the letting and management of premises.

Direct discrimination is defined at section 13 of the Equality Act 2010. It states direct discrimination is treating someone less favourably than others where the less favourable treatment is due to a protected characteristic.

In housing, where direct discrimination is alleged, it's normally on the grounds of disability. A person is disabled if they have a physical or mental impairment which adversely affects them. The effect must be long term and substantial, and adversely affect their ability to carry out normal daily activities. The nature of the impairment is less significant than the effect it has on the person. In fact, strictly, there is no need for a formal medical diagnosis. In reality, to rely on disability discrimination in proceedings, medical evidence confirming the diagnosis and the effect of the impairment is needed.

Direct disability discrimination is defined at section 15 of the Equality Act. It prohibits treating a disabled person unfavourably where the treatment is because of something arising as a consequence of their disability. However, the treatment will not be unlawful if a landlord can show the unfavourable treatment is a proportionate means of achieving a legitimate aim.

Disability discrimination may arise in an anti-social behaviour case where a person's disability causes or contributes to them behaving anti-socially. A landlord that tries to evict them because of that behaviour will be unlawfully discriminating against them. That is, unless the landlord can show the eviction is proportionate. There is no need for the disability to be the sole cause of the anti-social behaviour. But the disability must be an effective cause of the behaviour.

If a landlord can show it was not aware of a person's disability, nor could it have been reasonably expected to know about the disability, any unfavourable treatment will not be unlawful. But where available information reveals a real possibility a person may be disabled, landlords must make appropriate enquiries regarding their disability.

In a rent arrears case, it may be discrimination to evict a disabled tenant due to arrears caused by their disability. For instance, if the tenant is unable to manage their finances due to a mental impairment.

Proportionality is similar to reasonableness, although the courts adopt a structured approach to assessing proportionality. The structured approach requires the court to consider all relevant circumstances when addressing the following questions:

- Firstly are the facts sufficiently serious to justify eviction.
- Secondly, is there a rational connection between the landlord's reasons and the objective of eviction.
- Thirdly, are there alternatives to eviction that would achieve the objective.

- Finally, an overall balancing exercise to assess whether the ends justify the means.

There are two types of indirect discrimination.

Firstly under section 19 of the Equality Act 2010. This arises where a landlord's provision, criterion or practice, sometimes referred to as a PCP, has a discriminatory effect. The provision could be a landlord's anti-social behaviour or rent arrears policy. It may require the landlord applies for possession when someone behaves anti-socially or falls into arrears.

If the arrears or behaviour is caused by a person's disability, eviction will amount to indirect discrimination if the following conditions are met:

- The landlord applies the provision universally to disabled tenants and to tenants without a disability.

- Applying the provision puts a disabled person at a particular disadvantage when compared to a person without a disability.

- It in fact puts the disabled person at a disadvantage.

- And the landlord cannot show applying the provision is a proportionate means of achieving a legitimate aim.

The structured approach to proportionality will be especially relevant when dealing with indirect discrimination under section 19. This is because it may seem reasonable to have a policy to bring proceedings when there is anti-social behaviour, where the policy is applied to persons with and without disability. However, if the person's disability has caused or contributed to the anti-social behaviour, it's particularly important to consider alternatives to eviction. And to also consider whether the ends justify the means.

Secondly, there can also be indirect discrimination under sections 20 and 21 of the Equality Act. In a housing context these provisions impose a duty on a landlord to make a reasonable adjustment in relation to a tenant or a household member's disability. The duty applies where a PCP puts a disabled person at a particular disadvantage when compared to a person without a disability. The duty requires the landlord to take reasonable steps to avoid that disadvantage. However, the duty only applies if the landlord has been asked to make the reasonable adjustment to avoid the disadvantage.

The failure to make a reasonable adjustment may arise where there has been a failure to provide appropriate tenancy support services. This could be where a disabled tenant requires support with applying for benefits to ensure rent is paid. Or where a tenant requires support with managing their behaviour to avoid any problematic behaviour.

The Public Sector Equality Duty

The final provision under the Equality Act which can be relevant in possession claims is at section 149. This section sets out the public sector equality duty which applies only to public authorities. It therefore applies to all local authorities. It also applies to PRPSHs acting in a public capacity.

The duty imposed by section 149 includes the following:

- To eliminate discrimination, harassment, victimisation and any other conduct that is prohibited by or under the Act (subsection 149(1)(a)).
- To have due regard to the need to advance equality of opportunity between individuals with and individuals without a protected characteristic (see subsection 149(1)(b)).

- To have due regard to the need to take steps to remove or minimise the disadvantages suffered by individuals where this is connected to their protected characteristic (see subsection 149(3)(a)).

- To take steps to meet the needs of those with a protected characteristic where these are different to the needs of those without a protected characteristic (see subsection 149(3)(b)).

- The steps involved in meeting the needs of disabled individuals that are different from the need of individuals who are not disabled includes, steps to take account of an individual's disability (section 149(4)).

- Also, by section 149(6) of the 2010 Act, complying with its public sector equality duty may involve a public authority treating some people more favourably.

Except that the public sector equality duty does not apply to marriage or civil partnership, it applies to all other protected characteristics. Although section 149(4) applies only to disability.

The Equality and Human Rights Commission ("EHRC") has published Services, Public Functions and Associations: Statutory Code of Practice. It elaborates on the requirements of fulfilling the public sector equality duty. As it is statutory guidance, it can be relied on as evidence in proceedings. If a party relies on it, the court must take it into account.

Another publication by the EHRC, the Technical Guidance on the Public Sector Equality Duty, also provides comprehensive details on what the duty entails. Although not statutory guidance, public authorities should only depart from it where there are good reasons for doing so.

The duty applies to all functions carried out by public authorities. So it includes formulating policies, as well as decisions made in individual cases. It therefore applies to decisions about whether to evict a tenant. The duty is intended to ensure that a public authority's functions are carried out with equality considerations in mind.

There are some additional and practical aspects of the duty. These include:

- The need to make inquiries regarding an individual's disability if available information reveals a real possibility they may be disabled.

- Exercising the duty with substance, rigour, and an open mind, and must not simply be a tick-box exercise.

- It is a continuing duty that must be considered throughout the entire possession proceedings, whether the claim is brought on mandatory or discretionary grounds. The duty therefore continues up to enforcement.

- It is good practice to have a written record that the duty has been considered.

A significant aspect of the duty is its procedural nature. Therefore, it is not a duty to achieve certain results. But having due regard to the matters in section 149 is a duty, and so that must be complied with

60 – HUMAN RIGHTS

By article 8 of the ECHR everyone has the right to respect for their home. A public authority must not interfere with that right unless it would be proportionate to do so. Interference may be proportionate if it is necessary to do so. For instance, if interference is in accordance with the law, is in the interests of the public safety and economic well-being of the country.

The right to respect for a person's home is not absolute because there are circumstances when interference is lawful. It is therefore a qualified right. An occupier's right to respect for their home must be balanced against a landlord's ownership rights to the property.

When carrying out the balancing exercise, the court applies the test of what is proportionate. All the factors relevant to reasonableness described at sections 47 and 57 above may also be relevant when assessing proportionality under article 8.

But in achieving that balance, the court will normally attach significant weight to a social landlord's ownership rights. Because a social landlord also needs the ability to manage its housing stock to accommodate those with the greatest housing need. Therefore, in most cases making a possession order is likely to be proportionate. Because an occupier without security of tenure has no private law rights to remain in their home, so a landlord's ownership rights are likely to prevail.

An article 8 defence may be dealt with summarily, and is at risk of being struck out unless it is seriously arguable.

61 – VARYING A POSSESSION ORDER

A tenant may have grounds to apply to set-aside a possession order after it's been made. And either party may also apply to vary a possession order. This section deals with varying a possession order. Applications to set-aside a possession order are dealt with in the next section.

Where a possession order has been made on discretionary grounds, the court has the power to vary it. This power can be found at section 85(2) of the 1985 Act, and section 9(2) of the 1988 Act. In each case the wording is similar. They state that at any time before an order is executed, the court may stay or suspend execution of the order.

This means where an outright possession order has been made, the court can replace it with a suspended possession order. But the court should suspend the order on appropriate conditions, unless doing so would cause exceptional hardship. Therefore, if replacing an outright order made due to rent arrears, the new order should be suspended on condition the arrears are repaid by instalments. Or in an anti-social behaviour case, the new order should be suspended on conditions regulating conduct.

These provisions can be relied on to vary the terms of a possession order that was originally suspended. For instance, an order may be suspended on condition a tenant pays instalments which are no longer affordable. The tenant can apply to vary the order, so it is replaced by a new suspended order with affordable repayments.

Similarly, a landlord may apply to vary a possession order. For instance, if a suspended possession order has been obtained due to arrears, but subsequently there is anti-social behaviour. A landlord may apply to vary the possession order. The variation may be to impose additional terms, for instance regarding conduct. Alternatively, the variation sought may be to replace the original suspended possession order with an outright possession order. It should also be noted the landlord may make this application even if the tenant has complied with the terms of the suspended possession order. So a suspended possession order obtained due to rent arrears will require the tenant to repay the instalments. If the tenant makes all the required payments, a landlord may still apply to vary the order on different grounds such as anti-social behaviour.

However, the court does not have power to vary a mandatory ground possession order to a suspended order. This is why such orders should make clear they have been made on a mandatory ground. Doing so will make clear later whether the court has power to vary the order. Unless an outright order expressly states it's made on mandatory grounds, the court should proceed on the basis it was made on discretionary grounds.

62 – SETTING ASIDE A POSSESSION ORDER

Where an order is made in a party's absence, they may have grounds to apply for the order to be set-aside. In most cases it's the defendant-tenant who makes the application, but any party may make an application. Therefore, if the claimant fails to attend and the claim is dismissed, it may apply to set-aside that order.

Applications to set-aside court orders are governed by CPR 39.3. A party who makes an application needs to satisfy all of the criteria under that rule.

The criteria are as follows:

- That the applicant acted promptly when they found out an order had been made.
- The applicant had a good reason for not attending the hearing.
- The applicant's case has a reasonable prospect of success.

There is no specified period within which the application must be made. The rule simply states the applicant must act promptly. Whether a party has acted sufficiently promptly will depend on the circumstances of the individual case. Therefore, a legally represented party may be expected to act more quickly than an unrepresented vulnerable tenant. Particularly as CPR PD 1A requires the court to make allowances for vulnerable parties. Making allowances includes taking into account that a person's vulnerability may affect their ability to act in a timely manner.

Whether the reason for not attending is justified is also likely to depend on the circumstances of the case. A party who didn't attend the hearing because they arrived at court late, may elicit less understanding than someone who was unwell. Particularly if the illness is medically certified.

When assessing the prospects of success, the test is usually that there's a realistic rather than a fanciful prospect of success. Which again, must be assessed according to the merits of the individual case.

In some cases, where the CPR 39.3 criteria isn't met a more flexible approach may be available. The court may be persuaded it's in the interests of justice to exercise its powers under CPR 3.1(2)(m). This allows the court to take any step or make any order to manage the case in accordance with the overriding objective. The power under CPR 3.1(2)(m) is wide enough to cover setting aside orders in certain circumstances. But this power is only likely to be used in exceptional cases; set-aside applications under CPR 39.3 is the standard approach.

63 – WARRANTS

Where a social landlord obtains an outright possession order, that may not be the end of the matter. A tenant is entitled to remain, even after the date for vacating stated in the order has passed. If they do so, the social landlord will need to enforce the possession order. Enforcement is carried out by the court's appointed bailiffs.

If a landlord wants to enforce a suspended possession order that has been breached, that enforcement is also by bailiffs.

The landlord needs to initiate enforcement by applying to court for an appointment for the bailiffs to carry out the eviction. The application should not be made until after the date the tenant is required to leave, as stated in the possession order. In other words, the landlord cannot pre-empt enforcement by applying earlier, in anticipation that the tenant will not leave.

The procedure is usually straightforward in cases where an outright possession order was made. It's also straightforward where a suspended possession order made due to rent arrears has been breached.

In these cases, the landlord's application must be made at the hearing centre where the possession order was made. Or, if the claim was transferred, it must be made to the hearing centre the claim has been transferred to.

The application must be made on the form N49.The relevant fee must also be paid. Where a suspended possession order for rent arrears is enforced, the landlord must state on the N49 form the amount of the arrears that are unpaid. Any warrant issued will be defective if this information is not included.

If the claim was started via PCOL and the landlord obtains a possession order, it may use PCOL to apply for a warrant of possession.

The court will send out a notice of the appointment giving the date and time of the eviction. This notice is often called a bailiffs' warrant. The tenant must be given at least 14 days' notice of the eviction date. Sometimes the eviction doesn't take place on that date. In which case, another appointment is made, when only at least 7 days' notice needs to be given of the further appointment. The court may extend or shorten the 7 or 14-day period. Or in some cases the court may order that no notice is required, but that is rare.

When the bailiff visits the property at the appointed date and time to carry out the eviction, this is called executing the warrant.

The landlord can obtain the warrant without the court holding a further hearing. Although, as explained below, there may be a court hearing if the tenant makes an application after receiving the warrant. This is dealt with in the next section.

The process to enforce a suspended possession order made on a ground that was not rent arrears is different. The landlord must first obtain the court's permission. To apply for permission, the landlord must submit an N244 Application Notice setting out the basis of the application. The application must be made in accordance with CPR 23.

By CPR 83.2(4), the court's permission is also needed where the possession order being enforced was made more than six years ago. These orders are sometimes referred to as stale. If the landlord obtains a warrant to enforce a stale possession order without first getting the court's permission, the warrant is invalid.

In most cases the court will decide whether to give the landlord permission without holding a hearing.

Once a warrant is obtained, it is valid for 12 months from the date the warrant is issued. Therefore, it cannot be executed if it is more than 12 months old. This applies to warrants obtained with or without the court's permission.

However, a landlord can request the court extends a warrant that is more than 12 months old. If the court does so, the maximum extension will be for 12 months at a time.

64 – SUSPENDING A WARRANT

A tenant may apply to suspend execution of a warrant if the possession order was made on discretionary grounds. This option is available whether the possession order was an outright or suspended order.

The application must be made before the warrant is executed. It's made by submitting an N244 Application Notice to court. There is some space on the N244 Notice to provide evidence supporting the application. But tenants may find it helpful to submit a witness statement with the application, explaining their circumstances, and attaching any relevant documents.

If the possession claim was started via PCOL, the tenant may also use PCOL to make an application to suspend the warrant. That is providing the application is made at least 5 clear days before the bailiff's appointment. The court will serve a copy of the application on the landlord.

These are sometimes last-minute applications, made shortly before the warrant is due to be executed. Therefore they may be insufficient time for a court hearing to deal with the application to suspend the warrant before it's due to be executed. If that is the case, a tenant may also ask for the warrant to be stayed. If a stay is granted, execution of the warrant is put on temporary hold, pending the outcome of the application to suspend the warrant.

The test the court applies when deciding whether to suspend the warrant is reasonableness. This is the same test the court applied when making the original possession order. Therefore, it could be difficult for a tenant to get a warrant suspended shortly after an outright order is made. Unless they can show there has been some change since the earlier judge found it reasonable to make an outright order. And a tenant who breached a suspended possession order may also need to satisfy the court that a second chance is justified.

Theoretically, until a possession order is executed, a tenant may make repeated applications to suspend a warrant. But if repeated applications are made within a short period when there has been no change in circumstances, it may not be successful.

Factors relevant to reasonableness when the possession order was made, may be relevant to reasonableness at the warrant stage. Sections 47 and 57 above deal with factors relevant to reasonableness.

The court has a wide discretion. And while they cannot go behind the earlier judge's findings, another judge is not bound by the previous order. So a judge may suspend a warrant even though an earlier judge made an outright order.

Because the application is decided based on what's reasonable, all relevant factors will be considered. That means where a tenant applies to suspend a warrant, a landlord may rely on additional matters that were not raised as part of the original possession claim.

This may happen where a landlord obtains a possession order due to rent arrears, the tenant applies to suspend execution, and the landlord opposes the application. In this situation, the court may allow the landlord to raise allegations of anti-social behaviour as part of its reasons for opposing the application. The court may allow this even if the landlord didn't obtain the possession order due to the anti-social behaviour.

Where a landlord wishes to rely on additional matters, the court will take the following factors into account:

- Evicting a tenant is usually only appropriate if a serious breach of the tenancy has been admitted or proved.

- An application to suspend a warrant is intended to be a summary process. This may make proving anti-social behaviour within that summary process impractical.

- A tenant is entitled to have proper notice of the allegations being relied on before the application to suspend the warrant is dealt with.

65 – SETTING ASIDE A WARRANT

There are wide powers under the 1985 and 1988 Housing Acts to vary a possession order and suspend a warrant. The powers are under sections 84 and 85 of the 1985 Act, and sections 7 and 9 of the 1988 Act. But these powers can only be used prior to execution of the warrant. Following which, the tenant's only option to re-enter is if the warrant is set-aside.

However, a warrant will only be set-aside in limited circumstances. Firstly, if the original possession order is set-aside, any warrant will automatically be set-aside too.

Secondly, if there has been an abuse of process or oppression in the execution of the warrant, it will be set-aside. Oppression is difficult to define because it can cover a wide variety of situations. But it normally arises where there has been palpable unfairness. For instance, there would be oppression where a tenant is misled into believing enforcement action has been cancelled. If because of being misled, the tenant doesn't take steps to suspend enforcement, and the eviction goes ahead.

Oppression is not limited to the landlord's conduct: it can extend to court staff if they mislead a tenant. For instance, if they mistakenly tell a tenant they cannot apply to suspend the warrant. Also, oppression is not limited to cases of bad faith. So there may be oppression where a tenant is innocently misled by the landlord or someone else. And that misrepresentation prevents them applying to suspend the warrant.

The application is made by submitting an N244 Application Notice to court. It is important to explain in the application why it's said there has been oppression or an abuse of process.

CHAPTER FIVE

SUCCESSION

66 – SUCCESSION TO A SOCIAL HOUSING TENANCY

As stated, social housing was originally intended to provide long-term, and potentially lifetime accommodation. In some situations, the accommodation may even be provided beyond the lifetime of the original tenant.

This is because the law allows for succession (or inheritance) by a family member. Where the 1985 and 1988 Acts refer to spouses and civil partners in relation to succession rights, the term also applies to an equivalent couple. An equivalent couple is a couple living together as if they were spouses or civil partners.

Prior to the legislative changes discussed below, there could only be one statutory succession.

Statutory succession applies to sole tenancies only, and not to joint tenancies. This is because survivorship applies in the case of joint tenancies. It means that where one joint tenant dies, the tenancy automatically vests in the surviving joint tenant or tenants. Where there has been survivorship, that is treated as a succession.

Assignment (i.e. transfer) of tenancies is not discussed in this book. But where one tenant assigns their tenancy to another person, the assignment is treated as if it was a succession.

Traditionally, compared to assured tenancies, secure tenancies provided greater succession rights, because succession to a secure tenancy was available to a wider category of family members.

As social housing has become more scarce, legislative amendments have restricted those statutorily entitled to succeed. Those amendments were introduced by the Localism Act 2011, which amended the succession provisions under the 1985 and 1988 Acts.

The legislative amendments came into force on 1st April 2012. The restrictions that were introduced only apply to tenancies created after that date.

Therefore, statutory succession to a secure tenancy that began on or after 1st April 2012 is dealt with at section 86A of the 1985 Act, and the current version of section 89 of the 1985 Act. Statutory succession to secure tenancies that began prior to that date are governed by the previous version of section 89 of the 1985 Act. The previous version of section 89 applies to older tenancies as a result of the transitional provisions. Finally, statutory succession to an assured tenancy is governed by section 17 of the 1988 Act.

This means there are effectively four different statutory regimes covering succession.

- Firstly, covering pre-April 2012 secure tenancies.
- Secondly covering post-April 2012 secure tenancies.
- Thirdly covering pre-April 2012 assured tenancies.
- Fourthly covering post-April 2012 assured tenancies.

Different rules may also apply depending on whether the tenancy is periodic or fixed term.

In addition to these rules, there are also the non-statutory or discretionary succession policies a social landlord may have.

Social landlords usually have policies allowing for succession that is more generous than the legislation provides. For instance, some may allow for a second succession, or allow someone to succeed if they moved into the property to provide care to the now deceased tenant. Such schemes are sometimes referred to as discretionary successions. Strictly speaking, where such tenancies are granted, they are new tenancies, not succession tenancies.

Each statutory succession regime is described in more detail below.

67 – PRE-APRIL 2012 SECURE TENANCIES

The changes introduced by the Localism Act 2011 do not apply to secure tenancies that existed before 1st April 2012. Therefore, the old succession rights still apply to tenancies that began prior to that date.

This section deals with the succession rights under secure tenancies created before 1st April 2012.

Under these tenancies, a person qualifies to succeed if:

- They occupy the property as their only or principal home.
- And at the date of the original tenant's death, they were the tenant's spouse, civil partner or equivalent partner.
- And the deceased tenant was not a successor.

Alternatively, another member of the original tenant's family is also qualified to succeed if:

- At the date of the original tenant's death, they occupied the property as their only or principal home.

- And they resided with the tenant throughout the 12 months prior to their death.

- And the deceased tenant was not a successor.

If there is a spouse or civil partner plus a family member who qualify to succeed, the spouse or civil partner's succession rights take priority.

The Housing Act 1985 contains an exhaustive list of a family member. Therefore, anyone who is not included in the list will not qualify for a statutory succession.

Family members under the Housing Act 1985 applies to:

- A spouse, civil partner, or an equivalent partner;

- A parent;

- Grandparent;

- Child, stepchild, or child of parents who were neither married nor civil partners;

- Grandchild;

- Brother;

- Sister;

- Uncle;

- Aunt;

- Nephew; or

- Niece.

Where the above relationships are as a result of marriage or civil partnership, they are treated as a relationship by blood. Siblings who share one parent are also included in the above definition.

Where all these conditions are satisfied, there will be a statutory succession. So the deceased tenant's secure tenancy vests in (or is automatically transferred) to the successor. Because this is an automatic process, the social landlord cannot prevent the succession.

68 – POST-APRIL 2012 SECURE TENANCIES

Where a secure tenancy began on or after 1st April 2012, a person qualifies for statutory succession if the following conditions are satisfied:

- That person occupies the property as their only or principal home at the time the tenant died.

- And that person is the spouse, civil partner or an equivalent partner of the deceased tenant.

A person would also qualify for statutory succession in the following circumstances:

- If at the date of the tenant's death the property was not occupied by the tenant's spouse, civil partner or an equivalent partner.

- The express terms of the original tenancy allow a succession to someone other than the spouse, civil partner or an equivalent partner.

- And there is someone who falls within the criteria allowing for succession under the express terms of the tenancy agreement.

The express terms of some tenancy agreements allow more than one succession. If so, and any other conditions for a further succession are satisfied, the tenancy will vest in the person who satisfies those conditions.

69 – PRE-APRIL 2012 ASSURED TENANCIES

The express provisions of the Housing Act 1988 only deal with succession to periodic assured tenancies. They do not deal with succession to assured fixed-term tenancies. If an assured tenant dies during the fixed term, their will or the rules of intestacy determine succession. These will determine whether there will be a successor, and if so who.

The rest of this section deals with the succession rights under assured periodic tenancies created before 1st April 2012.

Before 1st April 2012, if a sole tenant died, there would be a statutory succession to a person satisfying the following conditions:

- The person is the deceased tenant's spouse, civil partner or an equivalent partner.

- Immediately before the death, the tenant's spouse, civil partner or an equivalent partner occupied the property as their only or principal home.

- And the deceased tenant was not a successor tenant.

Where all these conditions are satisfied, there will be a statutory succession. So the deceased tenant's assured tenancy would vest in (or is automatically transferred) to the surviving spouse, civil partner or the equivalent partner.

The express terms of some tenancy agreements allow more than one succession. If so, and any other conditions for a further succession are satisfied, the tenancy will vest in the person who satisfies those conditions.

70 – POST-APRIL 2012 ASSURED PERIODIC TENANCIES

Like the pre-April 2012 provisions, the Housing Act 1988 deals with succession to periodic assured tenancies. But unlike the pre-April 2012 provisions, the Housing Act 1988 also deals with succession to some fixed-term assured tenancies. It deals with fixed-term tenancies granted for a period of not less than two years. Succession to post-April 2012 fixed-term tenancies are dealt with in the following two sections. This section deals with post-April 2012 periodic tenancies.

The post-April 2012 provisions preserve the pre-April 2012 succession rights of spouses, civil partners or equivalent partners. But the post-April 2012 amendments introduced additional provisions for statutory succession which only apply to social landlords, not private landlords.

The additional post-April 2012 provisions for statutory succession are as follows:

- The original tenant was a sole tenant.
- The original tenant has died.
- Immediately before the tenant died there was no spouse, civil partner or equivalent partner entitled to a statutory succession.
- The express terms of the original tenancy allow a succession to someone other than the spouse, civil partner or an equivalent partner.

- And there is someone who falls within the criteria for succession under the express terms of the tenancy agreement.

Where all the above conditions are satisfied, the assured tenancy vests in the person satisfying the criteria.

Where the express terms of the tenancy agreement provide for more than one succession, providing any other conditions for succession are satisfied, the tenancy will also vest in the person who satisfies those conditions.

As previously stated, where a tenancy vests in a person, the social landlord cannot prevent the succession.

71 – POST-APRIL 2012 ASSURED FIXED-TERM TENANCIES – SPOUSE, CIVIL PARTNER OR EQUIVALENT PARTNER

Where there is a statutory succession to a fixed-term tenancy, the statutory provisions take priority over any will or the rules of intestacy.

The conditions below apply to assured fixed-term tenancies granted for not less than two years by social landlords.

In such cases, there will be a statutory succession where the following conditions apply:

- The original tenant was a sole tenant.
- The original tenant dies.
- And immediately before they died their spouse, civil partner or equivalent partner occupied the property as their only or principal home.

Where all these conditions are met, the remainder of the fixed term vests in the spouse, civil partner or equivalent partner.

The express terms of some tenancy agreements allow more than one succession. If so, and any other conditions for a further succession are satisfied, the tenancy will vest in the person who satisfies those conditions.

72 – POST-APRIL 2012 ASSURED FIXED-TERM TENANCIES – SUCCESSION TO PERSONS OTHER THAN A SPOUSE, CIVIL PARTNER OR EQUIVALENT PARTNER

The conditions below apply to assured fixed-term tenancies granted for not less than two years by social landlords.

In such cases, there will be a statutory succession where the following conditions apply:

- The original tenant was a sole tenant.
- The original tenant dies.
- Immediately before the tenant died there was no spouse, civil partner or equivalent partner entitled to a statutory succession.
- The express terms of the original tenancy allow for a succession to someone other than the spouse, civil partner or an equivalent partner.
- And there is someone who falls within the criteria allowing for succession under the express terms of the tenancy agreement.

Where all these conditions are met, the remainder of the fixed term vests in the person entitled to succeed.

The express terms of the tenancy agreement may allow more than one succession. In such cases, providing all conditions for a further succession are met, the tenancy vests in the person who satisfies those conditions.

73 – COMMON ISSUES WITH STATUTORY SUCCESSION

The most common dispute that arises in statutory succession is regarding residency of the potential successor. This can arise as a dispute about the following:

- Whether the person lived at the property at all.
- If the person lived there, whether their occupation was as their only or principal home.
- Whether the person lived there for the necessary relevant period.
- Or whether the person lived with the deceased tenant as a spouse, civil partner or equivalent partner.

The potential successor is expected to prove they are entitled to succeed if the issue is disputed. One way of doing so is by providing official documentation addressed to them at the property during the relevant period. For example, bank or credit card statements, credit agreements, mobile phone or similar contracts, gym membership, GP or hospital letters, driver's licence, employer's letter, official letters from government bodies such as regarding tax or benefits etc.

Social landlords may make their own enquiries. Typically, they will check the electoral register, council tax records and information held by credit reference agencies.

Any combination of these documents and records may help build a picture of a person's connections to a property. These may also show whether a person has a connection or a stronger connection to another property during that time.

But the records may not be determinative of whether a person lived at the property, or simply used it as a correspondence address. It may also not show the nature of their occupation.

Where someone has more than one address, the place they regarded as home is likely to be their principal home. That could be where they keep their personal possessions, where they sleep most of the time, eat their meals, spend their leisure time (e.g. evenings and weekends).

Where a potential successor has difficulty obtaining official documentation, evidence from other people could be relied on. This could come from friends or relatives, but their evidence may not be seen as independent. Evidence from neighbours could also be helpful. Providing such evidence is a neighbourly thing to do. And that is consistent with the potential successor being resident and establishing that neighbourly connection.

If an official person such as a health visitor, carer or social worker, frequently visited the property, they may also provide useful evidence of who did or didn't live there.

Either way, where evidence from someone else is relied on, that should be provided as a witness statement, because letters are not treated as evidence. That person should also attend court to give live evidence at a trial. Otherwise, the court may attach limited weight to their evidence.

When it comes to the duration of the successor's occupation, this doesn't normally arise with spouses, civil partners or equivalent partners. That's because they only need to have lived with the deceased tenant immediately before their death. Other family members who need to establish residency over a period of time may also try relying on the above evidence to establish the duration of their residency.

But as every situation will be different, each will need to be assessed on a case-by-case basis.

Similar evidence may be helpful to demonstrate two people lived together as if they were spouses or civil partners. For instance, having joint bank accounts, loans or other credit, joint benefit claims etc. Or official organisations had them registered as a couple for instance employers and insurers.

It should also be remembered that spouses or civil partners who live in the same home may not necessarily be living as if they were spouses or civil partners. This can happen if they have separated but still share a home. Or one may be acting as a live-in carer, even after their relationship has ended.

74 – NON- STATUTORY OR DISCRETIONARY SUCCESSIONS

Most social landlords have non-statutory or discretionary succession policies. These allow a succession where, after the tenant dies, there cannot be a statutory succession under the 1985 or the 1988 Acts.

As previously stated, although they are referred to as discretionary successions, in reality they are the grant of a new tenancy. So in the case of local authorities, these schemes will form part of an authorities' allocations scheme, which decides which housing register applicants will be awarded a new tenancy. And there is an important distinction between a succession and granting a new tenancy. If there's been one statutory succession, for instance in relation to a pre-April 2012 tenancy, there cannot be a second statutory succession. Whereas if a new tenancy has been granted, it may attract statutory succession rights.

Social landlords may operate these schemes in relation to pre-April 2012, or post-April 2012, or both pre and post-April 2012 tenancies. Also, such schemes are entirely discretionary, so there is no requirement that a social landlord operates such as scheme. The RSH's Tenancy Standard envisages social landlords may have a discretionary succession policy, but it doesn't require them to have one.

It also means the social landlord has the discretion to decide who may qualify under these schemes. And most operate on the basis that the landlord may refuse to grant a new tenancy even if the relevant criteria is met.

As stated, the tenancy vests in a statutory successor when a tenant dies. So the successor, automatically becomes a tenant. That doesn't happen with a discretionary succession. The potential successor will only become a tenant if the landlord exercises their discretion favourably. Unless or until that happens, the potential successor is an unauthorised occupier.

In such a case, the landlord may find it fairly straightforward to evict them. The tenancy would no longer be an assured or secure tenancy. Nor would it be an introductory or assured shorthold tenancy. That's because those tenancies require the tenant to occupy the property as their only or principal home. The deceased tenant cannot fulfil that condition. Therefore, the tenancy no longer has the statutory protection afforded by the 1985 or 1988 Acts. Instead, the deceased person's tenancy would continue to as an unprotected tenancy. Or it may be referred to as a common law tenancy. Again, because it isn't governed by statute but by common law.

A social landlord will still need to take certain steps to lawfully terminate the common law or unprotected tenancy. The first step is that the landlord must serve a notice to quit. The notice to quit must be served on the personal representatives of the deceased tenant. The personal representatives are the executors of the deceased tenant's will. If the tenant died intestate (i.e. without making a will), the personal representatives will be administrator of the deceased's estate. In some cases, there is no one acting as either executor or administrator. If that happens, the notice to quit must be served on the Public Trustee. The relevant fee must be enclosed when serving the notice to quit on the

Public Trustee. The landlord must also deliver a copy to the deceased's last known address, which in most cases will be the property itself.

The notice to quit must comply with the requirements set out at section 32 above.

The occupier will also have the protection afforded by section 3 of the 1977 Act. This means, if they stay after the notice to quit expires, the landlord must obtain a possession order to evict them. However, the landlord will not need to prove a statutory ground, because the person is an unauthorised occupier. So serving a valid notice to quit is a sufficient basis for the court to grant a possession order.

Providing the landlord follows the correct procedure, the court will make a possession order. That is, unless the occupier has a public law defence available to them.

CHAPTER SIX

TERMINATION BY THE TENANT

75 – TENANT GIVING UP POSSESSION

In most cases where possession is contentious, it's the landlord trying to recover possession from a tenant.

However, there are some points to consider when a tenant wishes to give up possession of their property. For instance, a tenant is bound by the terms of the tenancy until it is brought to an end. Therefore, it means the tenant remains liable for rent while there is a tenancy.

One way a tenant can end their tenancy is by serving a notice to quit. Most tenancies granted by social landlords contain provisions about how a tenant brings the tenancy to an end. If so, the tenant must comply with them.

If a periodic tenancy agreement does not deal with this, the tenant needs to serve a notice to quit on the landlord. This applies whether the tenancy was originally granted as a periodic tenancy or becomes a statutory periodic tenancy. The notice to quit must end on the last day of a period of the tenancy. It must also comply with section 5 of the Protection From Eviction Act 1977. Except that it does not need to contain the prescribed information. A social landlord may have a standard form that a tenant can complete that gives the required notice.

If a sole tenant provides an invalid notice to quit, the landlord can nevertheless accept it. If the landlord accepts the invalid notice, it will bring the tenancy to an end. But different rules apply to an invalid notice to quit served by one joint tenant, as set out below.

A tenant who wishes to bring their flexible tenancy to an end must give the landlord at least four weeks written notice, and specify in that notice, the date the tenancy will end.

The date given in the notice must be the last day of a period of the tenancy (i.e. the date a notice to quit would expire).

But if a tenant doesn't comply with these requirements, the landlord can dispense with the requirements, and accept the invalid notice as if it were a valid notice to end the tenancy.

Providing two further conditions are satisfied, the flexible tenancy will end on the date given in the tenant's written notice.

The two further conditions are that the tenancy will end on the date in the written notice if there are no rent arrears, and the tenant has not breached the terms of the tenancy in any material way.

With any tenancy under the 1985 or 1988 Act, if one joint tenant serves a notice to quit, it will bring the tenancy to an end for both joint tenants. This will happen even if the other joint tenant did not know or agree to the notice being served. But if one joint tenant serves an invalid notice to quit, it will only end the tenancy if all parties agree. That means all joint tenants and the landlord must agree to the invalid notice bringing the tenancy to an end.

MORE BOOKS BY LAW BRIEF PUBLISHING

A selection of our other titles available now:-

'A Practical Guide to Estate Administration and Crypto Assets' by Richard Marshall
'A Practical Guide to Managing GDPR Data Subject Access Requests – Second Edition' by Patrick O'Kane
'A Practical Guide to Parental Alienation in Private and Public Law Children Cases' by Sam King QC & Frankie Shama
'Contested Heritage – Removing Art from Land and Historic Buildings' by Richard Harwood QC, Catherine Dobson, David Sawtell
'The Limits of Separate Legal Personality: When Those Running a Company Can Be Held Personally Liable for Losses Caused to Third Parties Outside of the Company' by Dr Mike Wilkinson
'A Practical Guide to Transgender Law' by Robin Moira White & Nicola Newbegin
'Artificial Intelligence – The Practical Legal Issues (2nd Edition)' by John Buyers
'A Practical Guide to Residential Freehold Conveyancing' by Lorraine Richardson
'A Practical Guide to Pensions on Divorce for Lawyers' by Bryan Scant
'A Practical Guide to Challenging Sham Marriage Allegations in Immigration Law' by Priya Solanki
'A Practical Guide to Legal Rights in Scotland' by Sarah-Jane Macdonald
'A Practical Guide to New Build Conveyancing' by Paul Sams & Rebecca East
'A Practical Guide to Defending Barristers in Disciplinary Cases' by Marc Beaumont
'A Practical Guide to Inherited Wealth on Divorce' by Hayley Trim
'A Practical Guide to Practice Direction 12J and Domestic Abuse in Private Law Children Proceedings' by Rebecca Cross & Malvika Jaganmohan
'A Practical Guide to Confiscation and Restraint' by Narita Bahra QC, John Carl Townsend, David Winch
'A Practical Guide to the Law of Forests in Scotland' by Philip Buchan
'A Practical Guide to Health and Medical Cases in Immigration Law' by Rebecca Chapman & Miranda Butler

'A Practical Guide to Bad Character Evidence for Criminal Practitioners by Aparna Rao
'A Practical Guide to Extradition Law post-Brexit' by Myles Grandison et al
'A Practical Guide to Hoarding and Mental Health for Housing Lawyers' by Rachel Coyle
'A Practical Guide to Psychiatric Claims in Personal Injury – 2nd Edition' by Liam Ryan
'Stephens on Contractual Indemnities' by Richard Stephens
'A Practical Guide to the EU Succession Regulation' by Richard Frimston
'A Practical Guide to Solicitor and Client Costs – 2nd Edition' by Robin Dunne
'Constructive Dismissal – Practice Pointers and Principles' by Benjimin Burgher
'A Practical Guide to Religion and Belief Discrimination Claims in the Workplace' by Kashif Ali
'A Practical Guide to the Law of Medical Treatment Decisions' by Ben Troke
'Fundamental Dishonesty and QOCS in Personal Injury Proceedings: Law and Practice' by Jake Rowley
'A Practical Guide to the Law in Relation to School Exclusions' by Charlotte Hadfield & Alice de Coverley
'A Practical Guide to Divorce for the Silver Separators' by Karin Walker
'The Right to be Forgotten – The Law and Practical Issues' by Melissa Stock
'A Practical Guide to Planning Law and Rights of Way in National Parks, the Broads and AONBs' by James Maurici QC, James Neill et al
'A Practical Guide to Election Law' by Tom Tabori
'A Practical Guide to the Law in Relation to Surrogacy' by Andrew Powell
'A Practical Guide to Claims Arising from Fatal Accidents – 2nd Edition' by James Patience
'A Practical Guide to the Ownership of Employee Inventions – From Entitlement to Compensation' by James Tumbridge & Ashley Roughton
'A Practical Guide to Asbestos Claims' by Jonathan Owen & Gareth McAloon
'A Practical Guide to Stamp Duty Land Tax in England and Northern Ireland' by Suzanne O'Hara
'A Practical Guide to the Law of Farming Partnerships' by Philip Whitcomb
'Covid-19, Homeworking and the Law – The Essential Guide to Employment and GDPR Issues' by Forbes Solicitors
'Covid-19 and Criminal Law – The Essential Guide' by Ramya Nagesh

'Covid-19 and Family Law in England and Wales – The Essential Guide' by Safda Mahmood

'A Practical Guide to the Law of Unlawful Eviction and Harassment – 2nd Edition' by Stephanie Lovegrove

'Covid-19, Brexit and the Law of Commercial Leases – The Essential Guide' by Mark Shelton

'A Practical Guide to Costs in Personal Injury Claims – 2nd Edition' by Matthew Hoe

'A Practical Guide to the General Data Protection Regulation (GDPR) – 2nd Edition' by Keith Markham

'Ellis on Credit Hire – Sixth Edition' by Aidan Ellis & Tim Kevan

'A Practical Guide to Working with Litigants in Person and McKenzie Friends in Family Cases' by Stuart Barlow

'Protecting Unregistered Brands: A Practical Guide to the Law of Passing Off' by Lorna Brazell

'A Practical Guide to Secondary Liability and Joint Enterprise Post-Jogee' by Joanne Cecil & James Mehigan

'A Practical Guide to the Pre-Action RTA Claims Protocol for Personal Injury Lawyers' by Antonia Ford

'A Practical Guide to Neighbour Disputes and the Law' by Alexander Walsh

'A Practical Guide to Forfeiture of Leases' by Mark Shelton

'A Practical Guide to Coercive Control for Legal Practitioners and Victims' by Rachel Horman

'A Practical Guide to Rights Over Airspace and Subsoil' by Daniel Gatty

'Tackling Disclosure in the Criminal Courts – A Practitioner's Guide' by Narita Bahra QC & Don Ramble

'A Practical Guide to the Law of Driverless Cars – Second Edition' by Alex Glassbrook, Emma Northey & Scarlett Milligan

'A Practical Guide to TOLATA Claims' by Greg Williams

'A Practical Guide to Elderly Law – 2nd Edition' by Justin Patten

'A Practical Guide to Responding to Housing Disrepair and Unfitness Claims' by Iain Wightwick

'A Practical Guide to the Construction and Rectification of Wills and Trust Instruments' by Edward Hewitt

'A Practical Guide to the Law of Bullying and Harassment in the Workplace' by Philip Hyland

'How to Be a Freelance Solicitor: A Practical Guide to the SRA-Regulated Freelance Solicitor Model' by Paul Bennett
'A Practical Guide to Prison Injury Claims' by Malcolm Johnson
'A Practical Guide to the Small Claims Track - 2nd Edition' by Dominic Bright
'A Practical Guide to Advising Clients at the Police Station' by Colin Stephen McKeown-Beaumont
'A Practical Guide to Antisocial Behaviour Injunctions' by Iain Wightwick
'Practical Mediation: A Guide for Mediators, Advocates, Advisers, Lawyers, and Students in Civil, Commercial, Business, Property, Workplace, and Employment Cases' by Jonathan Dingle with John Sephton
'The Mini-Pupillage Workbook' by David Boyle
'A Practical Guide to Crofting Law' by Brian Inkster
'A Practical Guide to Spousal Maintenance' by Liz Cowell
'A Practical Guide to the Law of Domain Names and Cybersquatting' by Andrew Clemson
'A Practical Guide to the Law of Gender Pay Gap Reporting' by Harini Iyengar
'NHS Whistleblowing and the Law' by Joseph England
'Employment Law and the Gig Economy' by Nigel Mackay & Annie Powell
'A Practical Guide to Noise Induced Hearing Loss (NIHL) Claims' by Andrew Mckie, Ian Skeate, Gareth McAloon
'An Introduction to Beauty Negligence Claims – A Practical Guide for the Personal Injury Practitioner' by Greg Almond
'Intercompany Agreements for Transfer Pricing Compliance' by Paul Sutton
'Zen and the Art of Mediation' by Martin Plowman
'A Practical Guide to the SRA Principles, Individual and Law Firm Codes of Conduct 2019 – What Every Law Firm Needs to Know' by Paul Bennett
'A Practical Guide to Adoption for Family Lawyers' by Graham Pegg
'A Practical Guide to Industrial Disease Claims' by Andrew Mckie & Ian Skeate
'A Practical Guide to Redundancy' by Philip Hyland
'A Practical Guide to Vicarious Liability' by Mariel Irvine
'A Practical Guide to Applications for Landlord's Consent and Variation of Leases' by Mark Shelton
'A Practical Guide to Relief from Sanctions Post-Mitchell and Denton' by Peter Causton

'A Practical Guide to Equity Release for Advisors' by Paul Sams
'A Practical Guide to Financial Services Claims' by Chris Hegarty
'The Law of Houses in Multiple Occupation: A Practical Guide to HMO Proceedings' by Julian Hunt
'Occupiers, Highways and Defective Premises Claims: A Practical Guide Post-Jackson – 2nd Edition' by Andrew Mckie
'A Practical Guide to Financial Ombudsman Service Claims' by Adam Temple & Robert Scrivenor
'A Practical Guide to Advising Schools on Employment Law' by Jonathan Holden
'A Practical Guide to Running Housing Disrepair and Cavity Wall Claims: 2nd Edition' by Andrew Mckie & Ian Skeate
'A Practical Guide to Holiday Sickness Claims – 2nd Edition' by Andrew Mckie & Ian Skeate
'Arguments and Tactics for Personal Injury and Clinical Negligence Claims' by Dorian Williams
'A Practical Guide to Drone Law' by Rufus Ballaster, Andrew Firman, Eleanor Clot
'A Practical Guide to Compliance for Personal Injury Firms Working With Claims Management Companies' by Paul Bennett
'RTA Allegations of Fraud in a Post-Jackson Era: The Handbook – 2nd Edition' by Andrew Mckie
'RTA Personal Injury Claims: A Practical Guide Post-Jackson' by Andrew Mckie
'On Experts: CPR35 for Lawyers and Experts' by David Boyle
'An Introduction to Personal Injury Law' by David Boyle